Southern Living

HOUSE PLANS
CUSTOM-DESIGNED HOMES FOR THE SOUTH

Oxmoor House

Southern Living®
President & C.E.O.: Don Logan

Editor: Louis Joyner
House Plans Editor: Carolyn Rhodes
House Plans Coordinator: Lil Petrusnek
Homes Editors: Carole Engle, Linda Hallam, Deborah Hastings, Ernest Wood
Editorial Assistant: Rebecca Scoggins

Managing Editor: William T. McDougald
Copy Chief: Carol Boker
Art Director: Donovan Harris
Production Manager: Clay Nordan

Copy Editor: Kay Fuston
Staff Artists: Ann M. Carothers, Gabriele Cook, Carol W. Damsky, Charlotte Farnham, Julia D. Tyler
Assistant Production Manager: Wanda Butler
Production Assistants: Susan M. Emack, Vicki Nowlin Wade

Photographers: Ardon Armstrong, Bob Lancaster (senior), John O'Hagan (senior), Cheryl Sales

Editor, Southern Living: Gary McCalla
Executive Art Director: Thomas F. Ford
Executive Editor, Southern Living: Philip Morris

Creative Director: John Logue

Executive Vice President: James G. Nelson
Treasurer: Michael Murphey
Business Manager: Betty Robb Freeman
Production Director: Lawrence D. Rinehart

Circulation Director: Bill Capps
Circulation Manager: Hank Brown

Chairman: Emory Cunningham

Vice President, Advertising: James E. De Vira
National Sales Manager: Scott Sheppard
Southern Marketing Director: Burton Craige
Regional Advertising Managers: Kevin Lynch—New York, Dean Lord—Chicago, Vic Chieffalo—San Francisco, Steve Cummings—Los Angeles, Ed Fisher—Detroit, Glenn Majors—Dallas, Greg Keyes—Atlanta, Bill Dinan—Birmingham
Directory Advertising Manager: Martha Davenport
Research Manager: Patti Hendrix
Advertising Production: Tom Mitchell, Manager; Sharon Johnson, Assistant

Editorial Offices: Box 523, 820 Shades Creek Parkway, Birmingham, Alabama 35201
Southwest Editorial Office: 9020 II Capital of Texas Highway North, Suite 550, Austin, Texas 78759

Architectural Drawings: Roland Davis

All plans copyright, Southern Living, Inc., 1981, 1982, 1983, 1984, 1985, 1986, and 1987. Specific copyright information on individual plans available upon request.

© 1988 by Oxmoor House, Inc.
Book Division of Southern Progress Corporation
P.O. Box 2463, Birmingham, Alabama 35201

ALL RIGHTS RESERVED. No part of this book may be reproduced in any form or by any means without the prior written permission of the publisher, excepting brief quotations in connection with reviews written specifically for inclusion in magazines or newspapers.

Library of Congress Catalog Number: 88-60085
ISBN: 0-8487-0803-2
Manufactured in the United States of America

Cover
Supported by massive Doric columns, the overhanging roof forms a deep, shady gallery across the front of this Greek Revival-style house. For information on The Galleries, see page 12. Photo by John O'Hagan.

CONTENTS

4 READING YOUR HOUSE PLANS
A glossary of the terms, abbreviations, and graphic symbols we use on our house plans.

6 CHOOSE YOUR BUILDER—CAREFULLY
Suggestions on selecting the best builder for your new house, at a price you can afford.

7 HOW TO FINANCE CONSTRUCTION
Where to find the money for the lot, for construction, and for permanent financing.

8 TIPS ON BUYING A LOT
Tips on finding an affordable, buildable lot, in the right location.

10 PLAN BEFORE YOU GRADE
How to protect your site's trees from damage during construction.

HOUSE PLANS

12 Floor plans, renderings, elevations, and details for more than 60 of our best house plans.

INDEX & ORDERING INFORMATION

96 An alphabetical listing of our house plans, including page number and plan number. Also, what you need to know to order our plans by phone or by mail.

READING YOUR HOUSE PLANS

Working drawings, blueprints, plans—no matter what you call them, they are the important starting place for a new home. The plans are a form of shorthand for the architect or designer to communicate his ideas to the builder and the craftsmen who actually construct the house. And like shorthand, some of the lines and symbols may be hard for you to understand if you don't know the "language." To help, we've put together a list of frequently used abbreviations, a glossary of terms, and some of the more common graphic symbols used on our plans. Remember, though, that not all of the words or symbols will be found on every plan.

Terms

■ **Scale**—The various drawings that make up the house plans are drawn smaller than the full size of the actual house. For example, the floor plans are usually drawn to a scale of ¼" = 1'0". That means that ¼ inch on the drawing represents 1 foot. Details of parts of the house are usually drawn at a larger scale, such as ¾" = 1'0", 1½" = 1'0", or 3" = 1'0", or they may be drawn full-scale (actual size). Special architectural rulers, with these and other scales marked, are available at art supply stores or at a local blueprint company. Or you can use a standard ruler to measure any dimensions that are not shown on the plan.

■ **Foundation Plan**—Usually the first sheet of the working drawings contains the foundation plan and/or a basement plan. This is the plan that the builder will use for staking out the foundation on the lot. Since local conditions (slope of the site, soil types, local building codes) vary, it is important that your builder adjusts the foundation details to suit your specific site. Many of our plans are designed so that the crawl-space foundation can be changed to a full basement. Remember, too, that if you want to make any changes in the main living area that might affect the foundation, such as adding a fireplace or enlarging a room, you need to let the builder know before he starts on the foundation.

■ **First Floor Plan**—This plan shows the arrangement of rooms on the main level of the house. It also includes the location and width of window openings and door openings. Usually, the lighting plan is combined with the floor plan to indicate the location of the electrical outlets, lights, and switches. Floor plans for additional stories are usually found on separate sheets of the working drawings.

■ **Exterior Elevations**—These are front, side, and rear views of the house that illustrate how it will look from the outside. Because the orientation of the house on the site varies from situation to situation, our plans are labeled as front, left, right, and rear elevations. Some of our plans are designed with a specific site orientation in mind. For example, one elevation (usually the rear) may be designed with large glass areas that are supposed to face south to take advantage of the warming rays of the sun in winter. Changing the orientation of these plans could cause problems with increased solar heating in the summer.

■ **Interior Elevations**—These show the construction of walls that have built-in shelves or cabinets, such as in the kitchen, bath, family room, library, and bar.

■ **Sections**—In sections, the house looks as if it has been vertically sliced in half. The purpose of section drawings is to show the relationship of rooms, especially those located one above the other as in a two-story house. They also show raised ceilings, two-story areas, or other unusually spacious features.

■ **Wall Sections**—The construction of exterior walls, from the foundation up to the roof, is illustrated in these drawings. Wall sections will show the insulation of walls, floors, and ceilings, as well as the floor-to-ceiling heights.

■ **Finish Schedule**—Some plans include a chart that lists, room by room, the type of finish used on floors, walls, and ceilings. Other plans indicate the finishes on the appropriate floor-plan sheet.

■ **Door and Window Schedule**—Some of our plans list the sizes and types of doors and windows on a separate schedule. Others indicate the sizes and types directly on the floor plan or elevation. Usually, the size is indicated by four numbers, such as $2^6 6^8$. This means that the window or door measures 2 feet 6 inches wide and 6 feet 8 inches high.

Frequently Used Abbreviations

- C.D.X.—C&D grade exterior (plywood)
- COL—column
- CLO or CLOS—closet
- C.O.—cased opening
- C.M.U.—concrete masonry unit (concrete block)
- DIA—diameter
- DWG—drawing
- DN—down
- EXT—exterior
- FTG—footing
- GALV—galvanized
- GYP. BD.—gypsum wallboard
- HVAC—heating, ventilating, and air conditioning
- H.B.—hose bib
- H.D.—heavy duty
- INSUL—insulation
- N.I.C.—not in contract
- N.T.S.—not to scale
- O.C.—on center
- PR—pair
- P.T.—pressure treated
- RD—rod or round
- RND—round
- SH—shelf
- SHT—sheet
- SQ—square
- S4S—surfaced four sides (rectangular wood trim)
- S.F. or SQ. FT.—square foot
- SEC or SECT—section
- TRM—trim
- TRT'D—treated
- THK—thick
- T&G—tongue and groove
- W.H.—water heater
- WP—waterproof
- W/—with

ARCHITECTURAL SYMBOLS

⊖	DOUBLE-RECEPTACLE OUTLET	(hatched)	FINISH LUMBER
⊖●	SPECIAL-PURPOSE CONNECTION	(chevron hatched)	PLYWOOD
S	SWITCH	(cross hatched)	CONCRETE BLOCK
S³	THREE-WAY SWITCH	(dotted)	CONCRETE
⊗	VENT FAN	(irregular shapes)	STONE
◐	LIGHT/VENT/HEAT DEVICE	⌇⌇⌇	INSULATION
○	LIGHT FIXTURE	12/6 triangle	ROOF PITCH (6 IN 12 SHOWN)
⊠	ROUGH LUMBER		

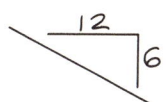

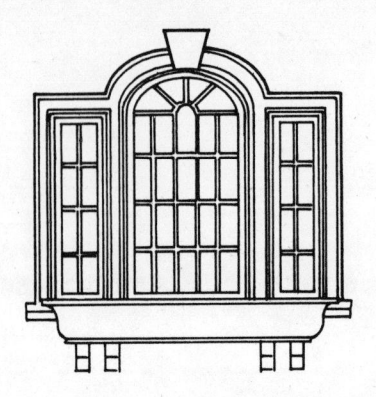

CHOOSE YOUR BUILDER— CAREFULLY

Of all the decisions that go into the construction of a new house, none is more important than selecting the general contractor.

Contractors coordinate the maze of permits, schedules, and subcontractors necessary for construction. They hold the ultimate responsibility of turning over the finished house to the client. Contractors may also sell or arrange the purchase of the lot or advise in its selection. In some instances, they can help arrange construction financing. And because they must translate plans into the finished house, the care contractors take is crucial for a successful job.

To begin your selection, compile a preliminary list of contractors. Check with friends, relatives, or business associates who have recently built houses, or drive by construction sites in residential neighborhoods. Local home-builder associations can provide lists of members and can advise whether certain builders specialize in large or small houses, and traditional or contemporary designs. And developers of new subdivisions will know which builders are active in their areas. Some subdivisions may allow only certain builders to work in that location.

After you have a preliminary list of contractors, check their references and backgrounds. Here's a list of things to consider:
- Can the builder give references from recent clients? Talk with the homeowners in private without the contractor or architect present. What do they say about the work? Would they recommend him? Would they choose him again? Did the contractor take longer than he said, and was it justified? And how clean was the crew? Did they clean up every day?
- In addition to clients, contractors should be able to furnish business and financial references. These should include suppliers the contractors do business with, such as lumber companies and paint stores.
- If licensing is required, make sure the contractor has a business license to operate in your area.
- Never hire a contractor who doesn't carry workmen's compensation and general liability insurance. To be extra safe, get a certificate of his insurance coverage and show it to the agent who carries your homeowner's insurance. In some cases, the homeowner may want to get additional temporary coverage.
- Make sure his company is permanently based in your area. The safest bet is to hire someone who has been in business at least three years and has a good track record.
- Does he use the same subcontractors for his jobs?
- Does the contractor have an acceptable credit rating with his bank?
- Does he pay the building-supply firm and subcontractors on time?
- Is he a member of the national and/or local Association of Home Builders?
- Have any complaints been filed against him with either the local Better Business Bureau or the local or state consumer-protection offices?
- Are any outstanding judgments filed against him? Is he currently being sued?
- Does the builder offer a warranty on the house, such as the Home Owners' Warranty (HOW)?
- When a contractor has been chosen, make sure he takes out the appropriate building permits.
- Get everything settled on paper before the work actually begins. Changing a project after construction begins can be costly and time-consuming.

With this preliminary research, you may want to choose a particular contractor and negotiate his fees. Or the final selection can be done through competitive bidding. In residential construction, preselected contractors are invited to bid. You should never let a contractor bid unless you are willing to let him build.

It is crucial that all contractors bid on exactly the same plan so fair comparisons can be made. And while the bid is an important factor in choosing the contractor, the lowest bid isn't necessarily the best because factors such as a reputation for workmanship need to be considered.

One payment method sometimes used in residential construction is known as cost-plus. This means the owner pays all costs of construction plus either a fixed fee or percentage of costs to the builder. Although cost-plus allows for changes during construction, any changes after the actual building begins can be costly. This is also true with a bid contract.

HOW TO FINANCE NEW-HOME CONSTRUCTION

The first step in building a house starts long before the basement is dug or the foundation is poured. It starts with that most crucial of building materials—money. And that means money for the lot and the construction and permanent financing.

Because the lot is the collateral for construction financing, it cannot be mortgaged. So in many cases, lots are purchased with cash. Or a homeowner with a large equity will take out a second mortgage on his current residence. This mortgage, like the first, is paid off when that house is sold.

An alternative in custom building is the builder who owns lots in a development. The builder may sell the lot, but more typically, he retains title during construction. The lot is then figured into the total selling price of the house.

Though it comes last, permanent financing—the long-term mortgage—must be arranged before the construction loan. The purchaser brings the lender the lot deed and his plans, along with an estimate from a builder of the total cost. The lender then qualifies the borrower for a loan as though he were purchasing an existing house. The borrower's financial background—income, savings, credit, and job history—are all considered.

Permanent mortgage loans are available from independent mortgage companies, mortgage subsidiaries of major commercial banks, and savings institutions. Today, both fixed- and adjustable-rate mortgage loans are made. Also becoming more popular are loans that are for a shorter term than the standard 30-year mortgages—such as 15-year mortgages. Another new option is the biweekly mortgage payment, which reduces the term because the principal is paid off sooner than with the usual monthly mortgage payments.

One of the most economical methods to finance a new house is a combination construction/permanent loan. The borrower pays interest only during the 6- to 12-month construction period. The construction loan is then paid in full, and regular mortgage payments on the permanent loan start automatically at the end of the construction period.

If the lender agrees to issue the mortgage, it's called a commitment from a permanent lender. The lender issues what is known as an approval or take-out letter to the borrower to use in arranging construction financing. Commercial banks and savings institutions are typical sources of construction loans.

As an alternative, a builder who has an established line of credit with a lender may arrange for the construction loan in his name. The interest paid by the builder on a construction loan is recognized as a legitimate building cost and is figured into the total price of the finished house. Either way, the actual cost of a construction loan is based on the amount of money (known as the draw) borrowed for a specific period of time. And the rate is usually a percentage or two above the prime lending rate. A construction loan fee, a percentage of the total loan, is also charged. Construction loans are usually six to nine months in term, and interest is paid on the amount of money outstanding.

Typically, draws are made after certain stages of the construction are completed. The money may be paid into the purchaser's account for disbursement to the builder. Or, depending upon the lender, the draws may be paid directly to the builder or to the subcontractors. When the house is completed, the long-term mortgage pays off the construction debt.

TIPS ON BUYING A LOT

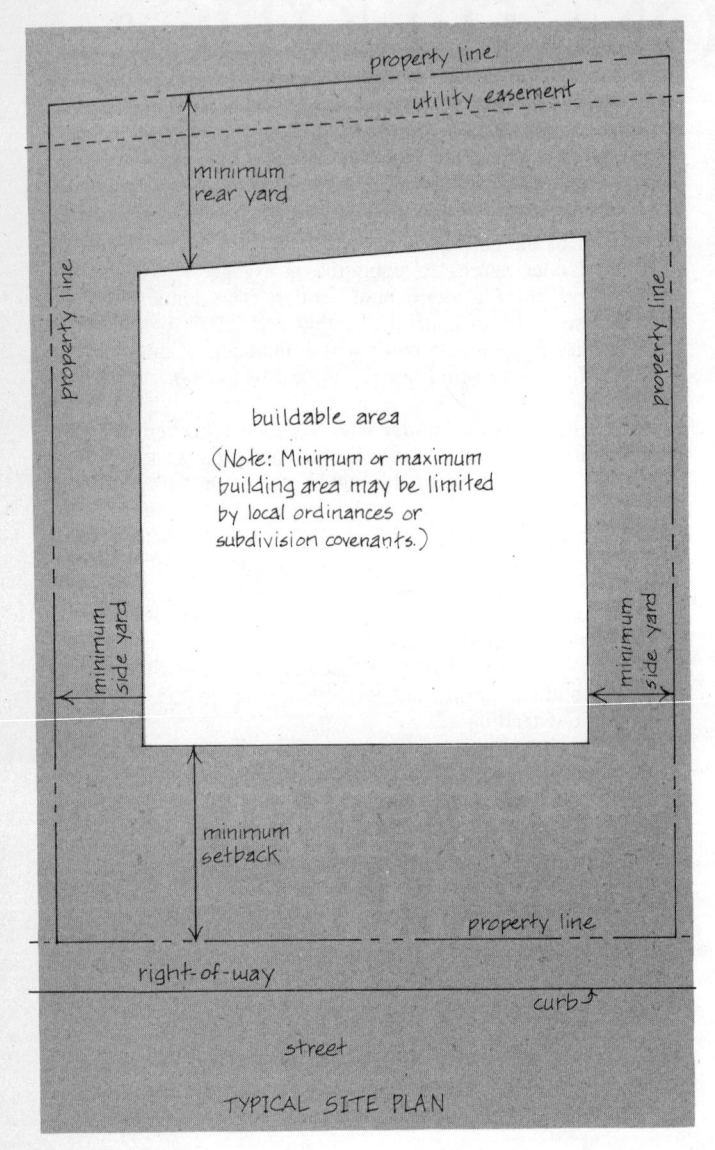

Just as in buying a house, selecting the right site for the house you plan to build can be an agonizing experience. In fact, many of the same considerations of buying a house are also important in choosing a lot. Remember, though, that selecting a lot involves a series of compromises. You probably won't be able to find that perfect spot, but at least you should try to consider both the good and bad points of each site you look at. Professional advice from a landscape architect can be a big help—especially if the site has some problems, such as steep slopes, poor drainage, or unattractive views. Many landscape architects will help select a house site for an hourly fee—ranging from $40 to over $100 an hour.

Location

The single most important factor in selecting a lot is location. And the best way to begin your hunt is to narrow down the choice of areas. If you are planning on building a new house in your present community, the choices are more clear-cut than if you are moving to another city or even changing to a different section of your present city. In the latter instances, a knowledgeable real estate agent can be a big help in evaluating the location.

An important factor to consider is proximity to shopping, schools, churches, playgrounds, and, of course, work. Finding out about the local schools is one of the most important tasks. Even if you don't have school-age children, the quality of the local schools will often affect property values and possibly the resale value of the house you build.

The price of existing houses in a neighborhood will also affect the resale value of houses built in that neighborhood; of course, it will affect the cost of lots in the neighborhood too. To be able to recoup your investment when you eventually sell, it's important that the cost of the lot plus the cost of the house you build is not appreciably greater than that of nearby houses. An expensive house in a neighborhood of modest homes will resell for less than that same house would in a neighborhood of comparable or more expensive homes.

In many cities, land use is controlled by zoning ordinances that set aside certain sections of the city for various residential, commercial, and industrial uses. A check with the local planning commission is a good way to be sure that the site you are interested in is indeed zoned for single-family houses. However, you need to be aware that zoning can be changed over the years. Some residential neighborhoods decline, and the zoning may change to permit rooming houses, apartments, or even commercial uses. Other neighborhoods improve, often after years of decline and neglect. New owners fix up older homes, and the usage changes back to single family. Often a drive through the neighborhood will give you an indication of this. Run-down houses and unkempt yards usually are an indication of an area in decline. On the other hand, well-maintained houses and yards show stability or an improving neighborhood. Generally, house and lot prices will reflect the neighborhood's direction. Check with a realtor to see if home prices have appreciated or gone down in the last year or two. Often the best bargains are in neighborhoods that have declined and are just starting back up. However, such bargains are somewhat risky. A safer bet would be a stable neighborhood or one that is well on its way to recovery.

Lots in new subdivisions also offer many of these same uncertainties. Will the subdivision develop the way it is intended to? Will any promised amenities (golf course, tennis courts, etc.) be built? What about schools and other public services? Usually, lot costs are low when a subdivision first gets started, and then increase (sometimes dramatically) as the subdivision grows.

One advantage of a new subdivision over an established neighborhood is the much wider choice of lots. But some subdivisions impose restrictive covenants on the minimum or maximum size house you can build, the exterior building materials you can use, exterior colors, and even the style house you can build. Some require you to build the house within a certain time limit, such as two years. Often an architectural review committee must approve each plan before construction. Generally, these restrictions result in a more attractive and more homogenous community. If the house you want to build meets the requirements, then the restrictions will actually help preserve your investment.

If you are planning on buying a lot in a rural area, be sure to check the availability of utilities (electricity, gas, water, sewer, phone, and television cable) and the cost of running utility lines to your house. Also, be sure to check on the proximity of schools and police and fire protection. And be aware of the growth patterns of any nearby cities. What seems like an idyllic country setting could be swallowed up by urban sprawl in just a few years. You should check to see who actually owns adjacent land and what plans they have for it.

The Lot

Once you have narrowed your choice of location, it's time to start looking at individual lots. Here are some of the questions you need to ask yourself.

■ Is the lot big enough for the size of the house considered? Remember that there are usually minimum front, side, and rear setbacks required that leave only part of the lot (the buildable area) for the actual house (see Typical Site Plan). Also, if a side driveway is needed, you will need to allow room for that and, if necessary, room for a turnaround. In many localities, a certain number of off-street parking spaces must be included. Sometimes these are required to be within the buildable area. Be sure to check with the local building commission or zoning board. Usually, the lot width, not depth, is the determining factor. You may be able to petition the local building commission for a variance to build closer to the street or to a side or rear property line.

■ Are there any restrictions or easements that could limit use of the property? Besides the design restrictions already mentioned, these could include utility easements (typically at the rear or along one side, these allow access of utility companies for service of power, telephone, or gas lines). You cannot build within the easement.

■ Are the surrounding houses and yards attractive and well kept? If you have children, will they find playmates within the neighborhood? Is there heavy traffic on nearby streets?

■ How is the site itself? A flat site is easier and less expensive to build on and offers more area for outside play, but may not be as interesting as a sloping lot. A sloping site can more easily allow for a basement and under-the-house parking. A lot that is sloping steeply may require both extensive site and foundation work.

Driveways and parking are often a problem with steeply sloping sites. But sometimes seemingly unbuildable lots can be bought for less. If you are considering a steeply sloped lot, one with large exposed rocks, or one with other problems, consult an architect, landscape architect, or engineer before buying. Remember, though, that the extra site work required can make a bargain lot more expensive than a lot that requires little site work.

■ Is it a lot or a swamp? Make sure the lot is not in a flood plain. If at all possible, take a look at the lot during and just after a heavy rain. This should point out any drainage problems. A lot that fills with water or one with a heavy waterflow through it could cause future problems with wet basements or soil erosion. Get professional advice.

■ What about trees? A heavily wooded lot will require at least partial clearing. Any large trees near the construction area will need to be protected during construction to prevent damage. Remember that pines are faster growing than hardwoods, but they are generally weaker and are more likely to topple or break in high winds. Also, evergreens block sunlight in the winter as well as in the summer, so they are less desirable from a solar heating standpoint. However, pines or other evergreens do make an effective windscreen in the winter, an important consideration in flat, open areas.

■ What other requirements might affect the site? Do you need parking for more than two or three cars? What about storage of recreational vehicles or boats? Do you want space for a large garden or a future swimming pool? Would you like a flat area for children to play or a large outdoor area for entertaining? Do you need extra room for any outbuildings, such as a guesthouse or workshop, and if so, where do you go locally to check on specific restrictions?

■ How much privacy is there? If this is an important consideration, remember that lots that slope up from the street generally offer more privacy than those that slope downward. On any lot, you can use the house and outbuildings (such as a garage) to help screen the rear yard from the street and from adjoining property. Fences and hedges can also add a sense of privacy. Corner lots, as a rule, offer less privacy.

■ Is it worth paying more for a lot with a view? It may be, but just remember that the character of the view may change over time (for example, the unspoiled valley may later turn into a shopping center). Before buying the lot, check to find out if there are any development plans for the land.

PLAN BEFORE YOU GRADE

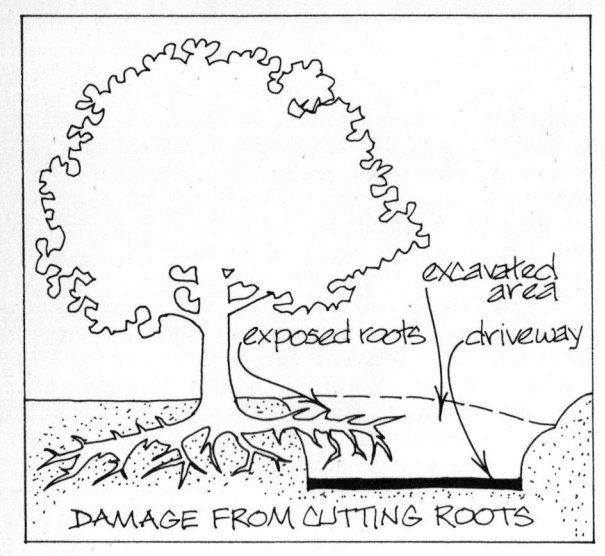

Cutting major roots to put in a driveway can seriously harm, or even kill, a tree.

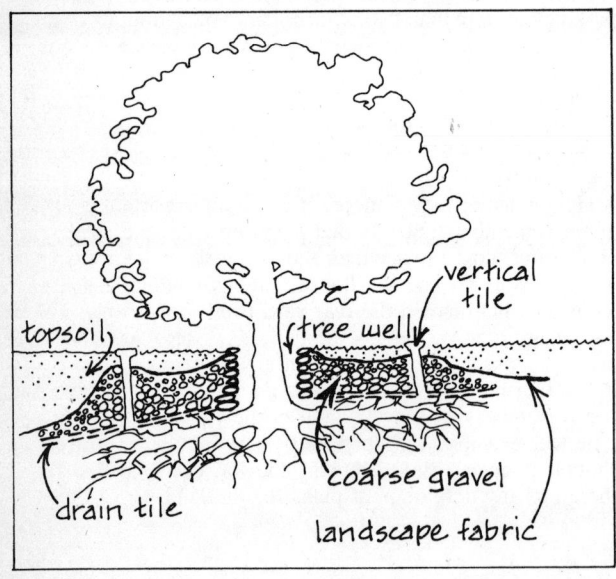

When the grade is to be raised by 1 foot or more, building a tree well and aeration field is the only way to save an existing tree.

In terms of aesthetics and property value, shade trees are one of a new home's most important assets. So it is disturbing to see a beautiful tree begin to die shortly after you move in. In most instances, the problem has nothing to do with you—it actually started when your homesite was being graded.

To understand how even slight grading can harm a tree, you must understand a little bit about a tree's root system. A tree uses tiny, hairlike feeder roots to gather nutrients and water. These roots are usually found in the top 18 inches of soil and often extend well beyond the tree's dripline. Their health depends on a delicate balance of soil moisture, microorganisms, and oxygen. Disturb any one of these elements and the whole system is thrown out of whack. Young trees can sometimes adapt to these changes, but older trees usually cannot.

One of the most harmful results of grading work is soil compaction. This occurs when heavy vehicles, such as bulldozers and dump trucks, are driven over tree roots or parked under trees. The extreme weight crushes the soil, squeezing out pore spaces and preventing penetration of water and air. Over time, this can cause a tree to decline.

Obviously, if your homesite has been graded for some time, there is little you can do. But if you have just bought a house, there are some precautions you can take.

If the site is freshly graded, there may still be time to unearth the covered roots, and then take steps (described here) to preserve the tree's health. And if construction hasn't begun, it's a good idea to visit the site and pick out any trees you want to save. Mark them clearly, and then place stakes around their driplines. Connect the stakes with fluorescent surveyor's tape, and let the contractor know that no vehicles are allowed inside the marked areas.

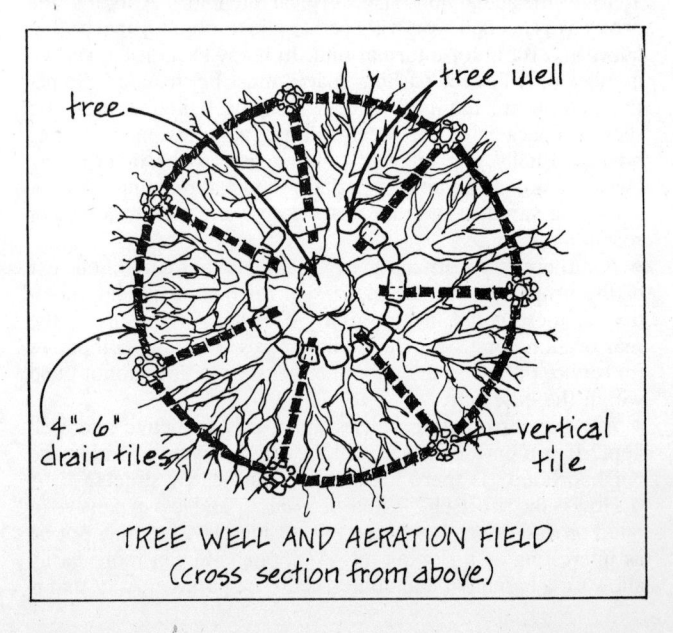

Bob Ray, a consulting arborist in Louisville, points out that heavy vehicles should not be parked anywhere on heavily wooded lots. Furthermore, the future parking area and driveway are the only areas where vehicles should be driven or the building materials delivered to and stored.

Don't Cut the Roots

The cutting of roots during excavation is another slow killer of trees. This most often occurs when soil is removed for roads and driveways. Many times, all the major roots on one side of a tree are severed. If the tree is young, numerous branches may die while it slowly adjusts; mature trees usually die. Cutting the roots of a large tree may also weaken its hold on the earth and make it prone to falling in windstorms.

If you must excavate close to a tree, try to keep the cut at least 15 feet away from the trunk. Remove the injured ends of mutilated roots, and quickly cover exposed roots with moist soil. If it is absolutely necessary to make the cut closer than 15 feet, you probably should remove the tree, and then plant a new one when grading is completed. This will save you the expense of having to cut the tree down when it dies a year or two after excavation.

Too Much Soil Is Deadly

Most of us don't consider soil to be dangerous to trees, but excess soil spread over tree roots is deadly. This happens when lots are leveled and the grade is raised around existing trees. The signs of soil-fill damage will soon appear. These include small, yellow leaves; numerous suckers along the trunk and major branches; many dead twigs; and large, dying branches.

This damage has several causes. First, piling soil over existing roots disturbs the operation of soil microorganisms, which break down organic matter into food for the trees. Second, atmospheric oxygen can no longer get to the roots. Third, toxic gases and chemicals, which may build up in the soil near the roots, can no longer escape into the air. Finally, the water table may be raised, which will result in waterlogging the roots.

Not all trees suffer from these effects to the same degree. Sugar maple, beech, dogwood, tulip poplar, pine, spruce, and most oaks are very sensitive. However, elm, poplar, willow, sycamore, and pin oak are more adaptable.

Once serious soil-filling damage shows up, it's usually too late to save the tree. The time to take action is before the grading is done. One method of raising the grade without harming the tree is by building a tree well to keep soil away from the trunk and allow the roots to get air, water, and nutrients.

If you have to raise the soil level more than 1 foot around the tree, you will also need to lay an aeration field of 4- to 6-inch tiles in a spoke-and-wheel pattern around the tree out to the dripline (see sketches). Lay the tiles on the original grade so that they slope away from the trunk (to keep water from flooding the tree). Next, lay a circle of tiles that connects the radial spokes. At the junctures of the spokes and circle, place vertical tiles that will extend to just above the new grade. Fill in over the horizontal tiles with between 6 and 12 inches of coarse gravel. Then lay a sheet of landscaping fabric over the gravel. Finally, spread 12 inches or more of good topsoil over the fabric, and smooth the soil until it conforms to the new grade.

Building a tree well and aeration field is not only a lot of trouble, it can be expensive. So before you decide to save a tree in an area to be graded, determine whether it is worth saving. Ask these questions: Is the tree healthy and vigorous? Is it a short-lived type (black locust, poplar, mimosa)? Is the tree weak wooded or weedy? Does it produce litter? Are there other trees nearby that serve the same purpose? You may decide that saving an old tree isn't worth the bother and expense needed to maintain it. Cutting it down and planting a new, more desirable tree may be wiser.

If you would like to learn more, contact the American Society of Consulting Arborists (Box 6524, Clearwater, Florida 33518), and ask them to recommend an arborist in your area.

12

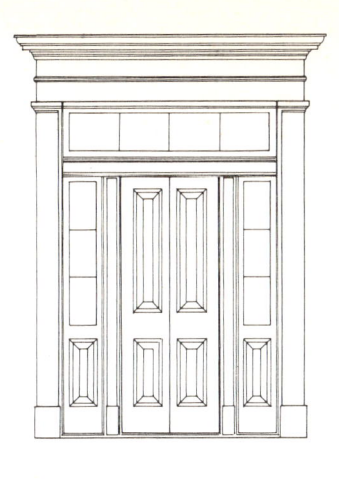

THE GALLERIES

A beautiful blend of the South's own raised cottage style and the more formal Greek Revival style, The Galleries offers elegance and comfort as well as traditional Southern charm.

The exterior design features simplicity and symmetry with four Tuscan columns topped by a simple dentil cornice supporting the front gallery. Sidelights and a transom surround the central entry, which is in turn flanked by long shuttered windows with overwindow moldings. Flush wood siding at the porches shows off the projecting architectural trim.

A climate-conscious plan, the house features front and rear galleries that offer areas for relaxing and also create a cool environment for the house.

Latticework at the foundation and carport lends a decorative yet practical touch; arched lattice panels set into the walls of the attached carport convert it into an airy breezeway.

The floor plan features a central foyer flanked by formal living and dining rooms, each containing a traditional mantel with marble hearth and facing. Wide cased openings between rooms combine with high ceilings (10 feet on the first floor and 9 feet on the second) to produce a spacious effect.

A comfortable family room contains a fireplace and a bookcase wall. The breakfast area is set into a bay, which projects slightly into the rear gallery. A utility room with powder room and laundry links house to carport.

Three bedrooms and two baths are upstairs, with the master suite featuring a dressing area/bath with large walk-in closet.

Working drawings for this plan include details for a small storage structure. Plans for The Galleries were designed for *Southern Living* by Architect Skip Tuminello, AIA, of Godfrey, Bassett, Maisel & Tuminello of Vicksburg and Jackson, Mississippi.

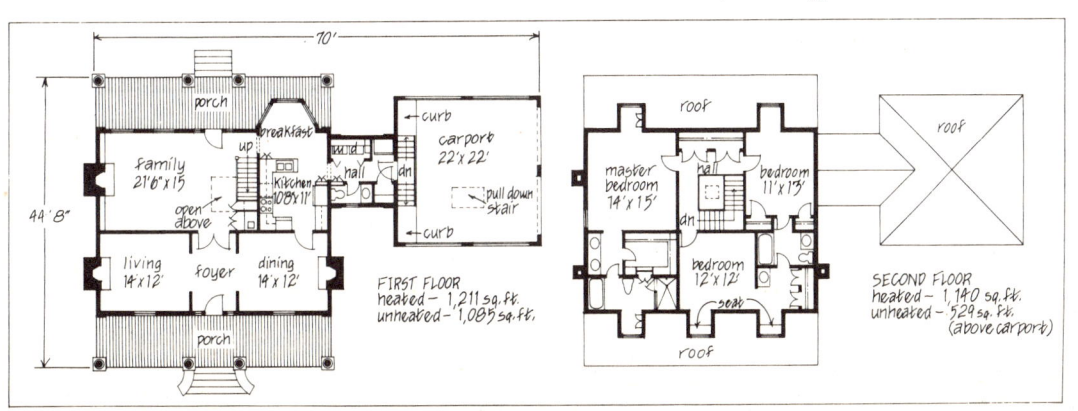

1105

VERNACULAR COTTAGE

Climate has always exerted a powerful influence on the architecture of the South. Before the advent of air conditioning, even the simplest houses were constructed with techniques that took both heat and humidity into account.

This raised cottage, designed by Architect Dean Winesett, AIA, of Hilton Head Island, South Carolina, combines many of these time-honored, common-sense solutions to the problems of living comfortably in the South. Inspired by raised cottages in Southern coastal areas and by the comfortable farmhouses of the interior South, the house's appealing vernacular style could work in a variety of locations.

The plan features a characteristic double-pitched roof, with the hipped portion covering galleries on three sides of the house. These galleries, or porches, once common features of Southern houses, serve as cool, transitional spaces between outdoors and indoors. Latticework between support piers allows cooling breezes to circulate beneath the three galleries. Windows extend to the floor to catch extra light and breezes.

Inside, the plan is simple, compact, and livable. A centrally located country kitchen with breakfast room forms the heart of the house. Running the depth of the house on either side of the kitchen are the master bedroom and a large great room with center fireplace. All lower-level rooms open directly onto the surrounding galleries.

The plan is composed of almost 1,900 square feet of heated space. Throughout the house, random nooks and pockets of space are enlisted for specific storage purposes, increasing the impression of space.

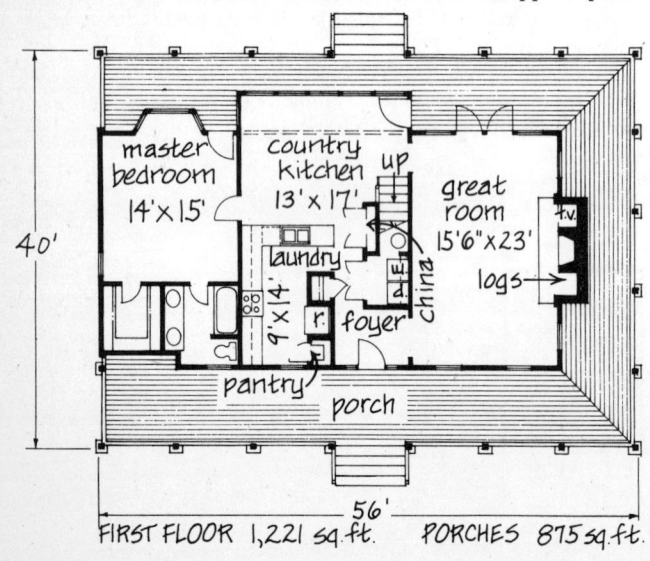

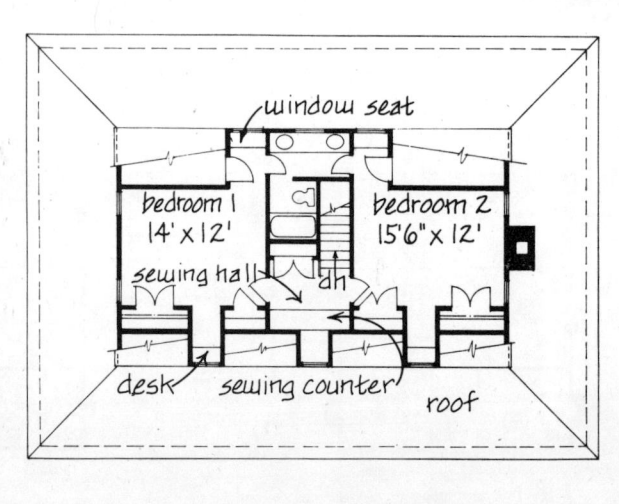

1101

FIRST FLOOR 1,221 sq.ft.   PORCHES 875 sq.ft.

SECOND FLOOR 662 sq.ft.

BUDGET BEACH HOUSE

Among the basic design features of this vacation house are simplicity and economy in a truly budget-type beach house efficiency.

Architect Ron Ward, of Phelps and Sullivan, Atlanta, designed a carefree weekend getaway. Short on pretense but long on fun, the compact plan contains about 750 square feet of heated space with about 650 additional square feet in deck space. Appealing to an active family, it has the charm and livability of a traditional summer cottage for beach or lake.

Built primarily of wood, the cottage's simple, straightforward construction is reminiscent of many turn-of-the-century beach houses. Perched atop poles with balloon framing above, the tiny cottage enjoys a lofty view of beach and sea. Storage space for a boat or parking space for a car is provided beneath. Use of natural materials ensures that the cottage will weather gracefully to become as much a part of the coastal landscape as a dock or a lighthouse. The simple gable roof over the living area and the hipped roof covering the deck are metal clad for heat reflection and durability.

The plan is simple, direct, and designed with nautical efficiency. All of the basics are provided for, as well as some thoughtful extras. For example, a private sleeping area in the loft has its own crow's nest deck. This deck can be used for stargazing and sunset watching.

An appealing feature of the design is its flexibility. Walls of the cottage lining the perimeter deck are standard doors, glassed for maximum visibility. These doors simply swing up, garage door fashion, and tuck neatly under the roof of the deck, stretching the main-floor living from about 530 square feet to almost 1,050 square feet. In addition to instantly expanding the living area, this system takes advantage of breezes and allows for absolute natural ventilation.

Although designed for the beach, this house could easily adapt to lakeside or mountain properties.

1102

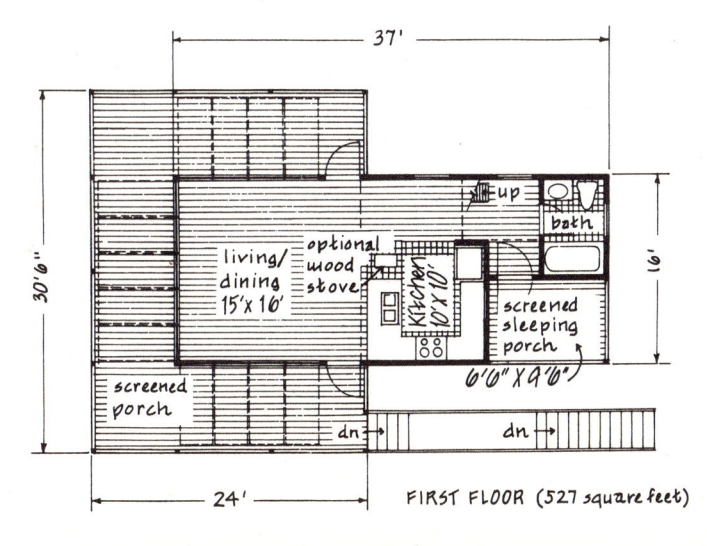

FIRST FLOOR (527 square feet)

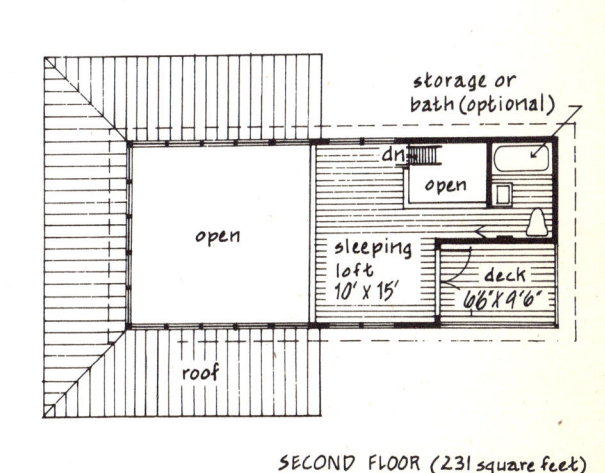

SECOND FLOOR (231 square feet)

A COURTYARD HOUSE

How do you retain the pleasures of suburban living on a small lot in the heart of town? This compact Courtyard House, designed by Tulsa Architect Jay Sparks, AIA, provides one good answer. It's a refreshing example of making every square foot count.

This house maintains a sense of privacy and offers pleasant garden views by turning inward around a courtyard.

Comprising approximately 1,800 square feet of heated space, with overall dimensions of about 42 x 76 feet, the house might be built on lots similar to those found in many older city neighborhoods—essentially leftover spaces with narrow frontages. The design may also be adapted for a zero lot line development by removing the windows on the side wall. And by rotating the plan, the house could be used on a conventional, wide suburban lot.

The design of the house is traditional, with gabled rooflines, clapboard siding, and multipaned windows. The house folds around the central courtyard, which is accessible from living area, kitchen/dining area, and master bedroom. Each of these areas borrows light, the illusion of space, and actual livability from the central court.

A second court, tucked into the ell formed by foyer and living room, further extends the living space and reinforces the garden feeling of the house. The separate foyer doubles as an energy-saving air lock.

The living room is spacious and appealing, with a vaulted ceiling lit by floor-to-ceiling windows and a clerestory window in the gable end. A freestanding fireplace divides living room and study. A dining area between the island kitchen and the garden court performs double duty as a breakfast area and a formal dining space.

The master bedroom has generous space, with separate sitting area, fireplace, walk-in closet, and compartment bath. The other two bedrooms feature built-in desks and lofts.

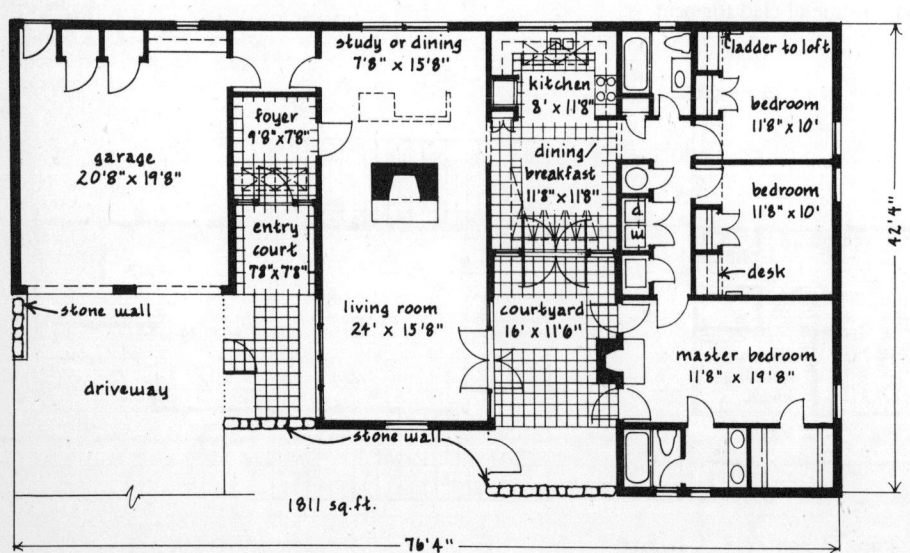

1104

CAPE COD, SOUTHERN STYLE

The simple good looks of the traditional Cape Cod cottage were so appealing that they were adopted in all parts of the country. Our version of the classic Cape Cod house has been "Southernized" and updated by Architect David Sullivan, AIA, of Phelps and Sullivan, Atlanta. It retains the simple massing and gabled rooflines of the original style, but it's been given an unexpected twist by being clad in stucco rather than clapboard or shakes, which lends a pleasing Southern look.

Crisp latticework detailing reinforces the subtropical Southern mood, while trellises at the entry and at the rear deck modify the effects of sun and heat, producing a bonus of appealing shadow patterns on house walls. Windows are recessed for coolness, creating a simple sculptural look, and are casement type to provide full ventilation.

The design offers elegance and variety in spite of its relative compactness. The plan is basically a 2,000-square-foot rectangle, but double-height spaces and strategic placement of corner windows visually expand the limits of the rooms and make the house appear much larger.

The recessed entry features semicircular steps and double doors flanked by sidelights. Inside, the foyer is designed as a separate, special room. A two-story space lit by sidelights and clerestory, it is allowed to retain its ceremonial function of welcoming guests and setting the stage for the house beyond.

The living room is airy and light filled and is partially open to the floor above. A window wall opens it completely to the rear deck, while skylights above admit additional light. Shading the living area from summer sun is a trellised deck.

The generous master bedroom comprises roughly a third of the downstairs plan. It is equipped with a large walk-in closet; a compartment dressing area/bath, which doubles as a powder room when guests are visiting; and a special feature—its own private latticed court.

The plan balances formality with function. For example, a separate dining room was included for special entertaining purposes, but could perform double duty as either library or study by the addition of perimeter bookshelves. The kitchen contains a pantry and a small office counter for bill paying and recipe storage. It opens to a separate breakfast room, and both rooms enjoy views to the deck beyond.

Upstairs, bedrooms are large, containing double closets, and are connected by a modified bridge that overlooks the foyer and part of the living room.

The architect recommends that the house be painted a light color for appearance and heat reflection, with latticework and trim defined in white. For passive solar heat gain, the house should be sited with the rear facing south.

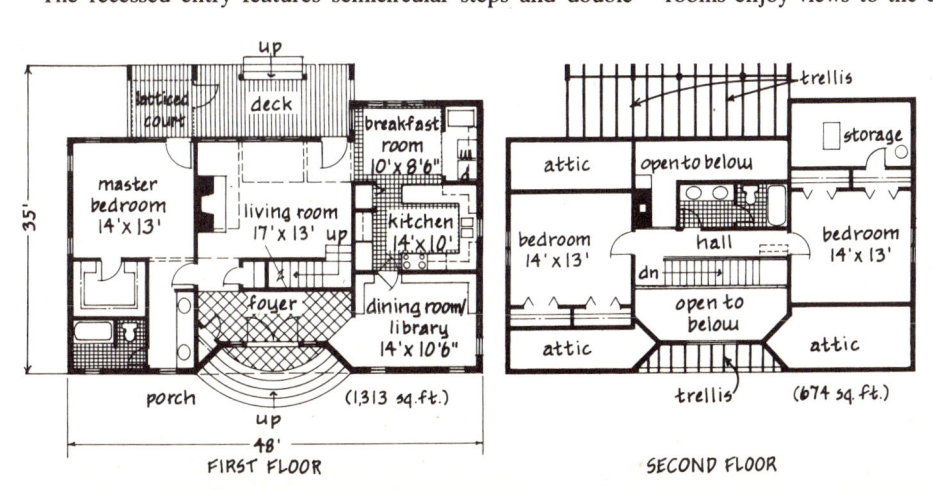

1117

CONTEMPORARY CABIN

Our Contemporary Cabin, designed by Architect William O. Moore, AIA, of Asheville, North Carolina, offers simple good looks and a flexible floor plan. Designed to meet the needs of a variety of families and to offer numerous conversion possibilities, the plan consists of close to 1,900 square feet if the lower level is left unfinished and almost 2,300 square feet with the lower level completed.

Although the house is contemporary, the inspiration for the design was largely traditional, with a rustic-cabin look the primary design objective. Exterior materials consist of all-natural finished wood with a corresponding use of natural materials, such as cedar and native stone, inside. A steep, gabled roof strengthens the traditional impression. Cantilevered decks extend the living space outside and create a tree house effect.

The plan comprises three levels linked by a circular staircase. This layering design allows for lower energy costs and saves on roof and foundation expenses. The floor plan is basically open and contemporary, with sleeping areas zoned for privacy. Plan variations can provide two, three, or four bedrooms and either two or three baths. The large space off the kitchen can be partitioned into a living room and separate dining room or left open, as shown.

The lower floor can be an unfinished basement, efficiency apartment, or a study/shop area. The architect suggests roughing in plumbing to this level and finishing at a later date.

The house is designed for steep hillside lots but can also be adapted to flat sites. With proper orientation, the design offers good potential for passive solar heat gain. Skylights embedded in the steeply pitched roof function as passive collectors and also visually extend the two-story space of the living room. The optional greenhouse off the dining room offers additional heat gain possibilities. The house may be entered through the main entry on the second floor or, for convenience, by means of the circular staircase at the lower level.

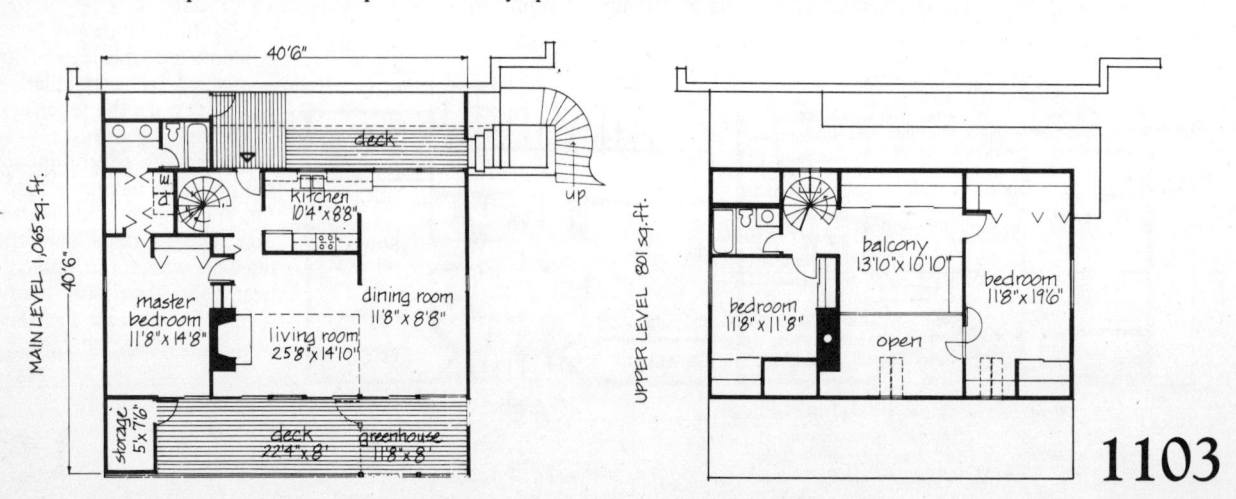

1103

A DECK HOUSE THAT'S SMALL BUT SPECIAL

Here is a witty and whimsical house and a half that proves the old saying that the whole is greater than the sum of its parts. It also demonstrates that smaller houses can be special and appealing.

Basically, the design consists of the main cottage, comprising about 1,000 square feet in its main level and loft, and a half cottage, comprising about 500 square feet in main level and loft. Separated and yet close enough for hospitality, the units are linked by a simple sunroom containing over 250 square feet, for a total size of about 1,750 square feet. There are also about 500 square feet in deck space.

The exterior design has gentle references to tradition in the form of gabled rooflines, board-and-batten siding, and fan windows set high into gable ends. An indoor-outdoor house, it sits atop its own deck, which is designed with an interesting angle to add to the fun. A simple balustrade defines the perimeter of the deck. Louvered, Bermuda shutters offer sun control and privacy and provide extra insulation in the winter.

Inside, the main house contains two bedrooms, each with its own bath, a kitchen, and living/dining area. The functional, galley-type kitchen contains laundry and mechanicals. First floor and loft are connected by a space-saving circular staircase.

The smaller half house contains a bedroom or study plus a small sitting area in the loft space above. Its separation from the main house would make it the ideal lodging for houseguests or perhaps for an older child. It might also be used as a studio retreat.

Linking the main house and the half house is a brick-floored sunroom with ventilating skylights.

Informal, and at the same time sophisticated, the house strikes a happy balance between privacy and sociability. Basically a funloving and unpretentious design, it would represent the perfect home for first-time buyers who might choose to build it in stages. Because of its inherent flexibility, it could just as beautifully suit the needs of an older couple with visiting children and grandchildren. For any age, it would make an ideal vacation house.

The best siting for passive solar heat gain would be with the extensively glazed elevation facing south for sunshine and garden views.

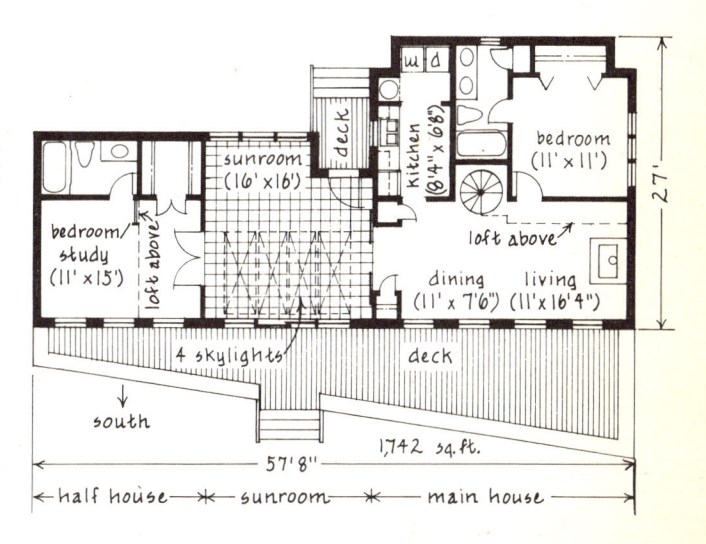

1106

MAIN LEVEL (1,238 sq.ft.)   UPPER LEVEL (580 sq.ft.)

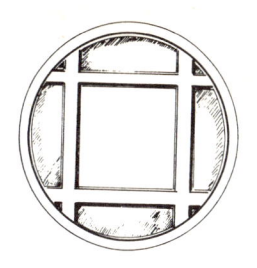

A COTTAGE OF STICKS AND STONES

From the peak of its high-gabled roof to the natural stone and cedar used in its construction, this rustic cabin house is pure Southern mountains. Although specifically designed with the rugged terrain and native materials of the Appalachian region in mind, the house could be beautifully sited on any well-wooded lot.

From the exterior, the house is appealingly simple, recalling the sturdy, primitive look of a log cabin. Use of local stone, stacked in a random pattern, and wood siding blend the house into its setting. Board-and-batten construction combines with simple post-and-rail detailing to give the house an old-fashioned, handcrafted look.

A small lookout porch at the front and a generous sitting porch at the rear provide views to the woods beyond. Completing the look of a compact mountain lodge are a steep, cedar-shingle roof and stone chimney.

Those who place a high value on comfort will be happy to find that the house's rugged impression ends at the front door. Beneath its sticks-and-stones exterior is a comfortable and informal plan, one that would serve a family equally well as a primary residence or as a second home. The house contains about 1,800 square feet of heated space and includes 3 bedrooms and 2½ baths.

A galley kitchen separates a light-filled breakfast room and a dining room. In the breakfast area, natural light lost to the overhanging porch roof is regained by the introduction of skylights. There's a spacious family/living room with stone fireplace, bar, and easy access to the rear porch.

Convenience and privacy were considered in the location of the master bedroom. Special design features include a cathedral ceiling and a circular window placed high in the gable.

Upstairs, two bedrooms and a shared bath occupy the space beneath the roof. Dormers with window seats offer additional lookouts for the occupants of the upper story.

The house includes a basement with space for two cars and a small workshop.

The house design is by Phillip Franks of Birmingham.

1108

CREOLE COTTAGE BLENDS TRADITIONS

In many areas of the Lower South, French and Spanish influences blended to form a unique house type—the Creole cottage. Borrowing freely from European styles, early settlers on the Gulf Coast gradually modified the design to adapt to the warm, humid climate.

Although born in towns along the Gulf Coast from New Orleans to Mobile, the Creole cottage also appeared in the interior South, where it was then influenced by the Greek Revival style. The symmetry, center-hall plan, and exterior chimney, shown here, are characteristic of this influence.

Like its predecessors, our Creole Cottage is raised slightly to place the living areas above the dampness of the ground. A steep gable roof sheds subtropical rains; the roof's pitch breaks slightly to cover a wide gallery across the front of the house.

Six slender columns support the gallery roof and a simple balustrade. Quaint cast-iron ventilators along the base of the house provide a distinctly New Orleans touch. Long, shuttered windows on the lower level combine with round-top windows in the gabled dormers to further define the regional look.

The house offers 1,650 square feet of heated space, with an additional 356 square feet in the deck and gallery. The modified center-hall plan contains a large combination living/dining room arranged to the left of the entry foyer. A master bedroom occupies most of the area to the right. A bath located at the end of the foyer allows access from the foyer as well as from the master bedroom.

A galley kitchen and adjoining pantry are placed at the rear of the house. A bright breakfast room/laundry is behind the pantry, forming an ell that encloses a deck. Accessible through French doors from both the breakfast room and the dining room, the deck adds a contemporary touch as well as extra dining and entertaining space. Two bedrooms and a bath occupy the upper story.

Our Creole Cottage was designed by Architect Bill Phillips, AIA, of Mobile.

1109

FIRST FLOOR (975 sq. ft.)

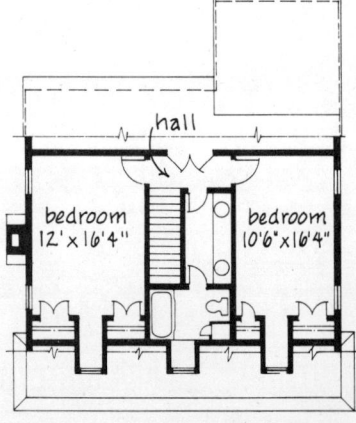

SECOND FLOOR (676 sq. ft.)

23

COASTAL COTTAGE

The coastal architecture of the South has character all its own, as this vernacular beach house clearly shows. Designed for *Southern Living* by Architect Edward J. Seibert, AIA, of Sarasota, Florida, it combines rambling, turn-of-the-century good looks with some special features that ensure comfort and energy efficiency.

The vernacular look is achieved in part by the veranda that encircles the main floor much like a ship's deck. It offers panoramic views toward land or sea and could be screened, if desired, for insect control. A skirting of latticework and a wooden balustrade provide old-fashioned carpenter detailing.

Proper siting helps direct sea breezes inside, while the deep veranda cools the air before it enters the house. To take advantage of this natural cooling system, the long axis of the house should be sited parallel to the beach.

Because it is specifically designed for the beach, low maintenance is a primary objective. Exposed exterior wood may be either a weather-resistant siding, such as cedar or cypress, or less expensive painted pine. The metal roof can be painted a light color to reflect the sun or be allowed to weather naturally.

Inside, the floor plan is simple and easygoing; the one-room-deep design throughout much of the plan allows for cross ventilation. As befits a vacation home, about half the square footage is for living and relaxing areas. Open planning and an absence of dividing walls underline the house's informality.

A large master bedroom, two smaller bedrooms, and a bath occupy the upper level. Six gabled dormers offer additional views to the outdoors. For extra sun control, these can be shaded with canvas awnings or with West Indies-type shutters.

A whole-house fan and slow-moving paddle fans pull air through the beach house; doors to the bedrooms and bath are louvered to permit both privacy and ventilation. An auxiliary heating and cooling system is included in the house plans.

With careful consideration for the ecology of the beach, the cottage is designed for siting behind the primary dune. A long boardwalk connecting house and beach minimizes disturbance of the sand dune and of the beach vegetation.

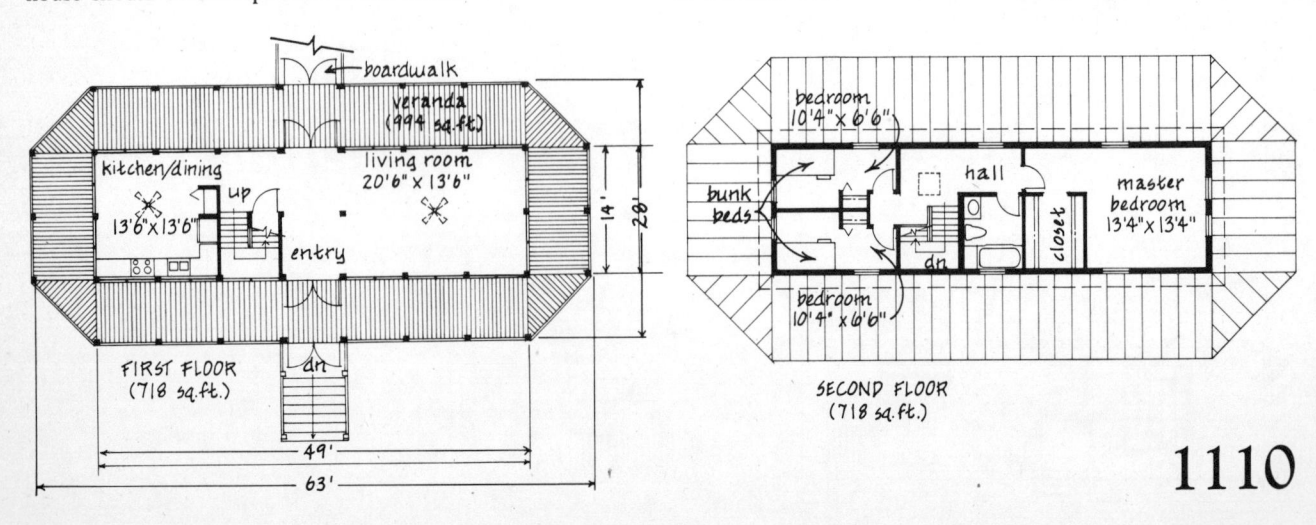

1110

MIXING SIMPLICITY WITH STYLE

Here's a compact, one-level house with enough style and flexibility to become either a first-time or retirement home or a lake or beachside cottage. Designed by Architect Dean Winesett, AIA, of Hilton Head Island, South Carolina, it's a simple but elegant little house, offering a blend of traditional and contemporary styling.

The house is raised slightly and sits atop a deck, which is cantilevered from the foundations to create a floating effect. Its hipped roof and deep overhangs covering galleries on all four sides of the house are reminiscent of early French-influenced houses in Louisiana. But the differences are just as marked. Subtle detailing and narrow sidelights at the corners of the house give a streamlined, contemporary effect. Rough-sawn cypress, angled and mitered for good looks, combines with a cedar shake roof to blend the house into its site. A perimeter gallery is accessible from all major rooms and is extended at the rear of the house to form a large projecting deck. A miniature version of this large deck greets guests at the entrance.

Glassed doors and windows are continuous on the rear elevation, allowing unrestricted views of garden, lake, or beach. Ideal siting for passive solar would be with the rear elevation facing south, although a particularly good view might dictate siting the house in a different direction.

Inside, the house is arranged simply and logically, with the floor plan divided into four parallel sections. More space in less square footage is gained by open planning, elimination of hallways, and a straightforward layout. Walls serve as dividers between living areas and, in some cases, as storage units. For example, a long fireplace wall with raised sitting hearth partitions secondary bedrooms from the living area. The wall separating living and kitchen areas houses a built-in china cabinet.

Sleeping areas are at opposite ends of the house with activity areas, such as kitchen, great room, and dining room, located between. A large master bedroom with walk-in closet and compartment bath runs the depth of the house on one end. There are three bedrooms and two baths and more than 1,500 square feet, excluding decks and galleries. The open plan and views to the outdoors make the house appear larger than it is.

The house is especially designed for a Southern climate. Roof overhangs shelter the galleries from rain and cool the air surrounding the house. Operating windows provide good cross ventilation.

Working drawings detail options for a boxed bay window in the master bedroom and dining room, as well as a cathedral ceiling over the great room, kitchen, and dining room.

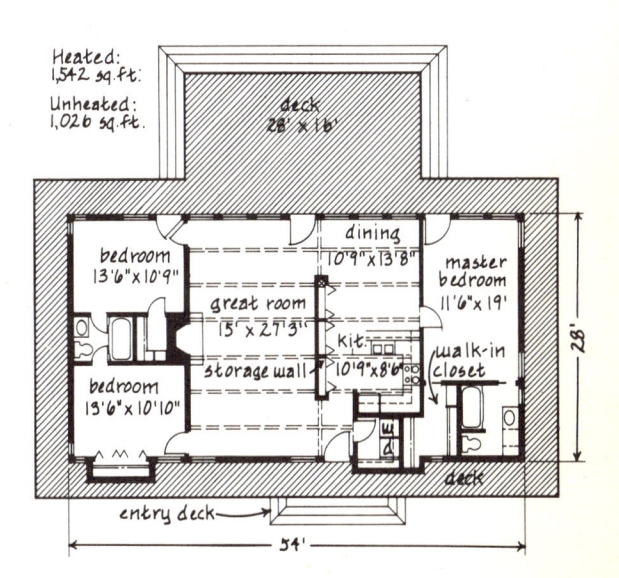

1113

BUILD A TRADITION

The garden district architecture of the South is well named. The houses found in these older, tree-lined sections of town invite the creation of gardens to set off the galleries, verandas, and terraces that are so much a part of their look.

This garden district house was designed for *Southern Living* by Watson, Watson, Rutland/Architects, Inc., of Montgomery, Alabama, to carry on the tradition of house and garden interaction. But it also includes some departures from tradition, which will make it practical for today. For example, it combines distinctive design with a relatively compact size. There are about 2,500 square feet of heated living area, with almost 600 additional square feet in galleries and veranda. Galleries and veranda are primarily for sociability, but they also serve as climatic buffers, tempering heat and light.

Multiple galleries, a hipped roof, and the careful use of stucco and lattice give the house its classic good looks. A wooden balustrade at the upper gallery has the look of decorative ironwork. The two-story center section of the house is set between wings.

As was often the case with older Southern homes, the front gallery receives the same attention to detail as do the interior rooms. Flush wood siding allows architectural trim at doors and windows to stand out in crisp relief. Upper-gallery windows are arched, and there's a classic fanlight over the front door.

Beyond the traditional exterior is an open, contemporary floor plan, creating a mood of relaxed formality. A double-height foyer steps down into a large living room. To the right of the foyer, a separate dining room overlooks the front gallery. Triple French doors in the living room lead to a columned veranda, which opens to a semi-enclosed rear garden. Since it is so focal, this garden might be treated formally with evergreens.

The right wing contains a kitchen with island work area, pantry, and small office counter. There's a separate breakfast room with boxed bay window, and beyond this, a laundry and utility bath. A latticed breezeway links the carport to the house.

The master bedroom occupies the left wing of the downstairs plan and includes its own private sitting porch. A connecting bath has walk-in closets, shower, and corner bathtub, plus private access to the rear garden.

Upstairs, two bedrooms share a connecting bath, with the front bedroom opening to the large upper gallery.

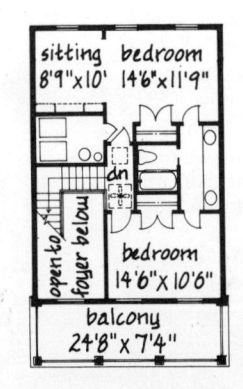

FIRST FLOOR (1,824 sq.ft.)   SECOND FLOOR (681 sq.ft.)

1111

A HOUSE FOR TOWN OR COUNTRY

The special appeal of a weekend resort and the year-round comfort and livability of a home in town—our cypress-and-stucco cottage offers exactly that by combining the best of town and country living and by presenting its owners with a life-style that can be either formal or relaxed.

Much of the home's charm derives from its simple, traditional lines. Raised on a foundation of whitewashed brick, the house features a hipped roof covered in wood shakes, multipaned "cottage casements," and a center chimney with well-detailed brick cap. Four boxed cypress columns support the recessed entry porch. Functioning wood shutters can be added to secure the house.

The floor plan is beguilingly simple and yet flexible enough to accommodate either town or country living. There are about 1,900 square feet of heated space, including three bedrooms, two baths, and a large living room/great room at the house's center. A vaulted ceiling and exposed beams over this central living area and in the master bedroom give a spacious, open feeling. Skylights on the rear pitch of the roof open the house to trees and sky without compromising the home's traditional looks. French doors and long transom-topped windows help open rooms. Wood-plank walls and whitewashed brick at the fireplace restate the country lodge look. The freestanding fireplace in the living room defines a small entry area.

There's a full-size kitchen with pantry and island work area, a breakfast room, and a separate dining room. A deep, L-shaped porch at the rear is for sitting and enjoying views of beach, lake, or simply a pretty garden.

The master bedroom is set apart from the main portion of the house in its own wing. It includes a vaulted ceiling, a window wall, and French doors opening to the sitting porch. Built-in bookcases frame a comfortable sitting area, and quarter-round windows flank a fireplace in the gable end.

Windows and doors are carefully placed for cross-ventilation. Wide, cased openings between rooms, a whole-house fan, and paddle fans in major rooms increase air circulation. Ceilings are 9 feet except in the living room and master bedroom.

The plans include construction drawings for an attached garage. Details are given for both a crawl space and a slab-on grade foundation.

Our cottage was designed by Phillip Franks of Birmingham.

1115

ALWAYS WANTED A GAZEBO? BUILD ONE OF OURS

Gazebos, belvederes, or summerhouses—no matter what you call these garden structures, they are special places to enjoy the beauty of the outdoors, providing shade from the sun and shelter from summer showers. The names alone evoke visions of picturesque gardens steeped in Southern tradition.

Here are six different gazebos in a broad range of styles to complement most residential settings: the **Chippendale**, with Georgian-inspired design; the **lathhouse**, for the traditional look of lattice; **rustic**, with a rugged, hand-hewn appearance; **Victorian**, displaying turn-of-the-century detailing; **contemporary**, showing clean, straightforward lines; and the **open-air option**, with a light, almost tropical feel. All have one element in common—they share the same basic structure—and all styles are detailed in these plans that we offer, for $45 per set, from which you can choose and build your own gazebo retreat.

The plans contain detailed construction information offering options for customizing the gazebo. The basic size of all six gazebos is 8 feet square within the posts, with a 10-foot-square roofline; this is an ideal size for residential application, providing enough room for comfortable furniture arrangement or even for a table and chairs for outdoor dining.

Three interchangeable floor choices are given: an 8-foot deck surface, an ongrade brick floor, and an oversize deck with steps wrapping each side. Various railings are illustrated, and all are the same size for design flexibility. Finishes and materials are the builder's choice.

If you have good woodworking ability and a fair knowledge of construction techniques, you should be able to understand these plans and be able to construct your own gazebo with some help from a friend. However, you can hire a carpenter. The cost for materials should range from $600 to $1,000. Labor cost should average about that or a little higher.

The Chippendale-style gazebo illustrated at right is located at the Birmingham Botanical Gardens on Lane Park Road in Birmingham. The gardens are open daily from dawn until dusk, and admission is free.

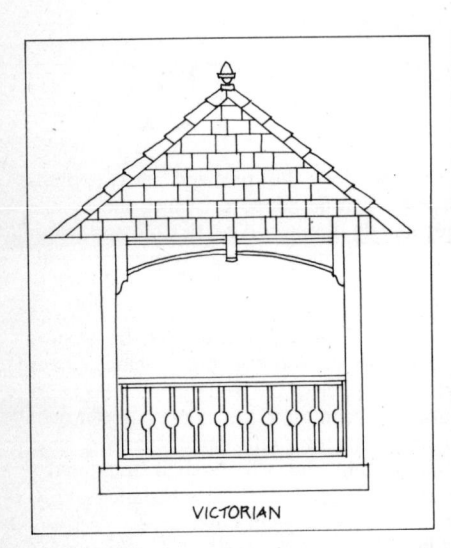

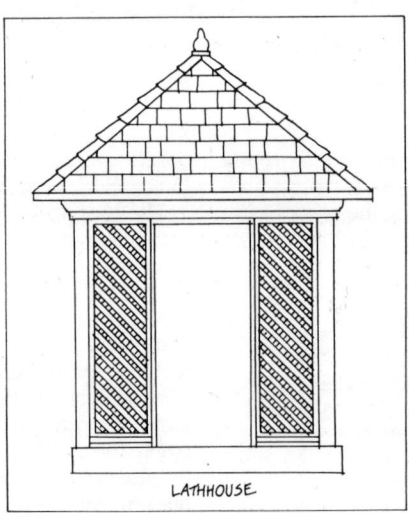

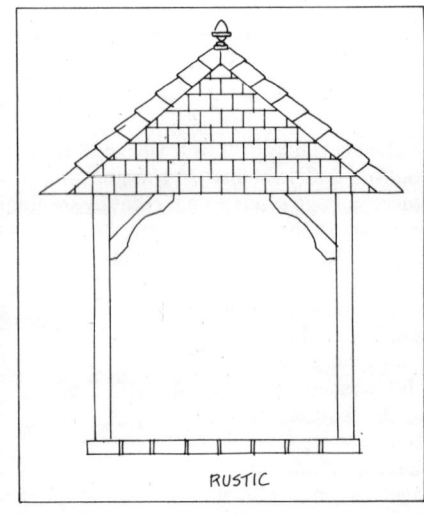

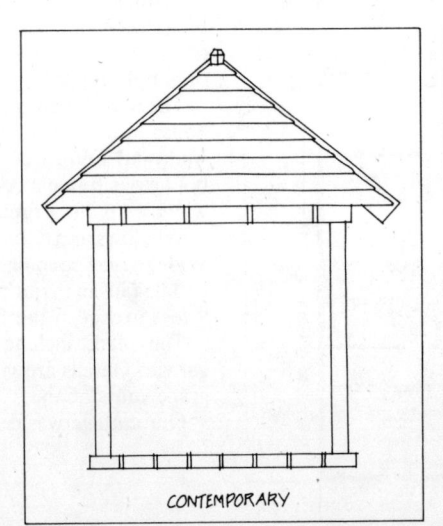

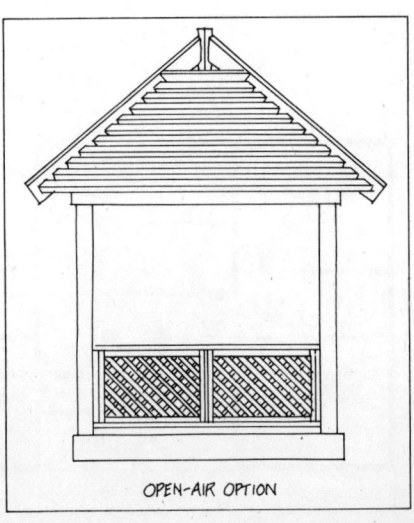

VICTORIAN

LATHHOUSE

RUSTIC

CONTEMPORARY

OPEN-AIR OPTION

1112

IT'S COUNTRY ENGLISH— IN TOWN

Our Country English Cottage is perfectly suited to in-town living. It meets the functional requirements of smaller sites, yet it maintains a sense of comfortable elegance. Designed by Architect Zachary W. Henderson, AIA, of Roswell, Georgia, the plan is derived from medieval English homes that often featured carriage houses convenient to the entry.

Borrowing from the English styles of the 17th and 18th centuries, the plan adapts architectural features long-favored in the South. The front doorway is detailed with fanlight, sidelights, and traditional wood moldings.

Behind the traditional exterior is an open, contemporary floor plan, creating a mood of relaxed formality. From the double-height foyer, a warm and inviting fireplace awaits in the grand room. Large in scale, this room is vaulted with skylights.

Reminiscent of the old Southern keeping room, the kitchen/breakfast area is spacious. A built-in desk, below-counter wine storage, and accessible pantry make the kitchen one of the house's most livable rooms.

For convenience and privacy, the master suite with large bath occupies its own wing on the main level. A screened porch offers a cozy sitting area and opens to the deck.

Upstairs are two bedrooms and a shared bath with separate vanities.

The plan offers about 2,600 square feet of living space. An optional basement plan details a fourth bedroom, bath, and recreation room.

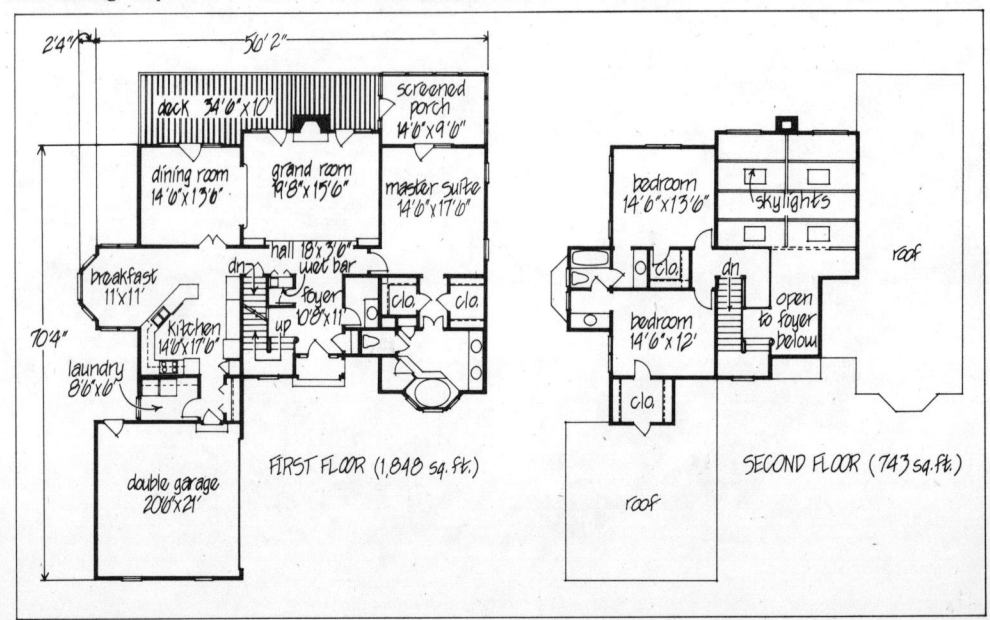

1172

A TEXAS-STYLE FARMHOUSE

Set between sturdy stone chimneys, our early Texas-Style Farmhouse carries useful lessons for today.

The roof is steeply pitched for shedding summer downpours, and it overhangs 12-foot-deep porches. Doors and floor-length windows give thorough cross-ventilation. Smaller "Texas windows" beneath the roof pull cool air into upstairs rooms.

Designed by Architect Barry Moore, FAIA, of Houston, the house is basic in the best sense, with rooms laid out in a simple, straightforward manner. Many of its details are adapted from historic Texas houses at Round Top.

The entry hall is wide and welcoming, derived from the open dogtrot of early Southern homes. At each end, screened double-door openings with transoms continue the tradition of a breezeway.

The dogtrot becomes part of a generous sweep of space between living room and dining room. Large cased openings give a long view of the twin fireplaces at the sides of the front rooms. A cozy inglenook off the living room holds a window seat and built-in bookcases.

The master bedroom is located in the L-wing at the back of the house. It features a vaulted ceiling with skylight, double walk-in closets, and an adjoining bath.

Upstairs are two large bedrooms and a shared bath, which includes double dressing areas, bathtub, and separate shower.

The plan contains about 2,600 square feet of heated space with another 1,150 square feet in porches.

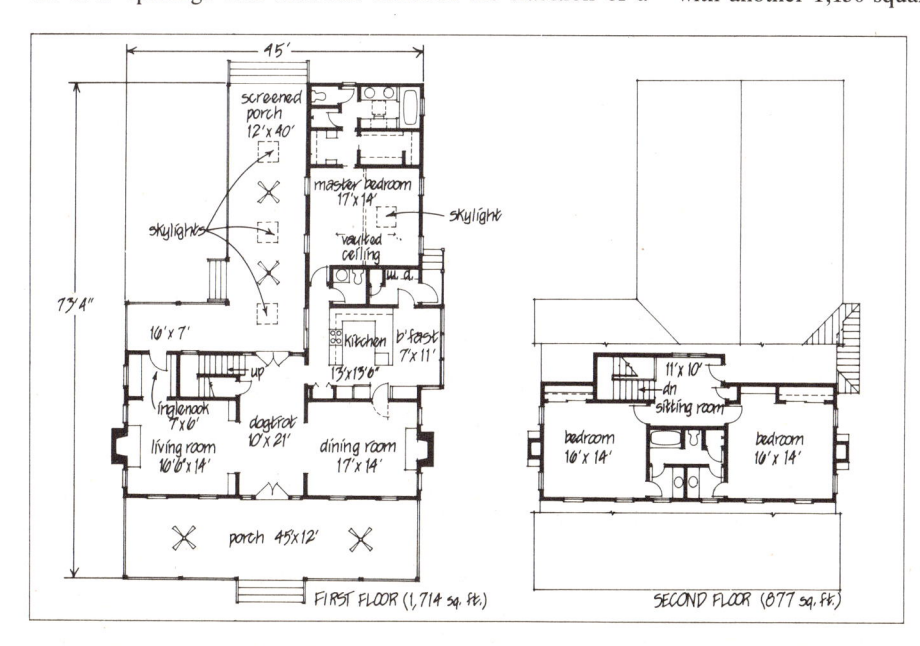

1169

32

COUNTRY GEORGIAN

Comfortable and expansive in the tradition of many old-fashioned Southern homes, our Country Georgian house offers an engaging blend of country comfort and formal architectural styling. Designed by Architect Dean Winesett, AIA, of Hilton Head Island, South Carolina, it's an easy and charming interpretation of the Georgian style, carefully adapted to the practical requirements of a warm, humid climate.

A familiar type in the coastal areas of Georgia and the Carolinas, the house is raised on a basement to keep it cool and dry. The basic design includes main house and wing and offers 4 bedrooms and 3½ baths in about 2,800 square feet of heated space. If budget or family size requires a smaller house, the master bedroom wing may be omitted, leaving a square footage of almost 2,400.

The house is of stucco, which might be painted a light, pastel color for heat reflection. The double-pitched roof is of standing-seam metal, which could be allowed to weather naturally or might be painted a dark green or oxide red as was often done in the past.

A spreading roof with deep overhangs and the placement of doors and windows create a natural cooling system. Gallery, screened porch, and sunroom ease the transition between outdoors and in and serve as comfortable sitting areas.

Parapet walls at each end of the main body of the house follow the lines of the steeply pitched gable roof, giving a sense of solidity and strength and reinforcing the distinctive coastal look. A gallery with a balustrade spans the front of the house, its six boxed columns supporting a simple cornice.

Inside, rooms are spacious with 9-foot-high ceilings downstairs. Double-door openings off the broad center hall open the house visually and to breezes. The master bedroom wing contains adjoining bath, walk-in closet, and a projecting bay. A glassed sunroom at the rear could serve as a sitting room for the master bedroom or as an extension of the breakfast room. Breakfast and dining rooms are roughly equal in size and will accommodate both informal family meals and formal dinners. The proportioning and placement of windows and doors will allow traditional furniture arrangements.

Three bedrooms, two baths, and a broad stair hall occupy the upper floor. Six dormers (three gabled and three shed) expand space and capture light for upstairs rooms. The lower level contains about 1,500 square feet in double garage and workshop.

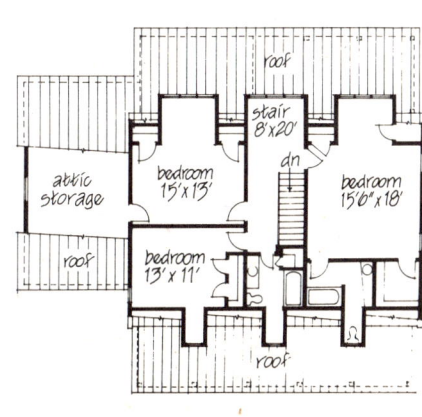

1116

A PLAN FOR INDOOR AND OUTDOOR LIVING

A two-bedroom house that offers the comfort and special features of larger, custom homes is hard to find, even though the two-bedroom market is growing steadily. Designed especially to meet that need by Architect Gerald Quick, AIA, of Raleigh, this house is stylish, livable, and flexible enough for either primary or vacation use.

The plan merges indoor and outdoor living areas, offering about 2,700 square feet of living space, with over 1,600 square feet indoors and close to 1,100 square feet in deck and courtyard. Window walls, skylights, and clerestory produce a bright, spacious effect and open the rear of the house to views of garden and sky. The front elevation is basically closed, with additional buffering from the street's sights and sounds provided by a brick-walled parking court.

Simple but well detailed, the house is of beaded-wood clapboard with brick trim. An arched Palladian fanlight at the rear and quarter-round "half-fan" windows flanking the fireplace add appealing traditional touches to what is basically a contemporary design.

Inside, conventional planning is used for bedroom and bath areas to ensure privacy; open planning is employed in living, dining, and entertaining areas of the house to maximize the sense of space. Steep, gabled rooflines offer space inside to vault ceilings and to include loft spaces, if desired.

Special features include a sun/garden room, a small enclosed space between the house and the rear deck. It can be opened fully for ventilation and might also be moved to the front of the plan for a more flexible sun orientation. A skylit dining room enjoys an open view of the rear deck and the garden beyond.

Since outdoor living is such an important part of the plan, the house is especially well suited for resort areas of the South. A large, private courtyard to the front of the house serves as a preliminary entry. Here, a brick, openwork, screen wall provides visual separation from the parking court and carries across the front of the house to form an extension of the living room accessible through glass sliders.

A small outdoor storage room for planters, hoses, and garden equipment is tucked into a corner of the entry courtyard. To the rear of the house a large wood deck provides an additional open-air living area.

Its design and plan make our two-bedroom house especially appropriate for use as a first house, retirement home, or vacation home.

1118

A TIDEWATER TRADITIONAL

The coastal Virginia Tidewater area produced one of the South's best loved architectural styles. The Tidewater house was basically a simplification of the English Georgian-style house, modified to suit the local climate, available building materials, and the skills of colonial craftsmen.

Our Tidewater Traditional plan was modeled after several of these early Virginia homes. Among them are the Red Lion Inn at Williamsburg and the Old Mansion in Caroline County. Architect Bill Phillips, AIA, of Mobile, Alabama, designed the Tidewater Traditional house for *Southern Living*.

The detailed brickwork includes jack arches over windows, corbeled chimney caps, and a molded water table below the first-floor level. Brick walls are laid in a Flemish-bond pattern. Mortar is finished in the colonial struck fashion to help create an impression of age for the exterior. Carpenter trim is simple but formal with modillion cornice dressing the eaves. A Chippendale railing in the Chinese trellis pattern borders the porch. The gabled roof with clipped corners, a familiar type in colonial Virginia, gives the house its distinctive profile.

At the entry, double doors are set beneath a brick lintel and six-light ribbon transom. Brass carriage lamps flank the door.

Inside, a long center hall doubles as a gallery when equipped with track lighting. Ten-foot ceilings lend volume to the main-floor rooms. Brightness and warmth are ensured by the plan's three fireplaces and by generous stretches of window walls along the rear.

A double-door opening between living and dining rooms allows them to serve as one large space. There's a large open kitchen with island work area and a box bay window breakfast space. Separate pantry and laundry link the house to its attached double garage.

The left part of the downstairs plan is given entirely to the master bedroom and adjoining bath, dressing area, and glass-walled garden sitting room. A long outdoor gallery, placed in the ell defined by the house's back walls, serves as a breezy summer living room with views of the formal garden.

The house is designed to relate closely with its brick-pathed garden, inspired by English examples and adapted to local climate and plant materials. We've included a planting plan for a boxwood and perennial garden with our construction drawings.

Upstairs are two bedrooms and a shared bath. Loft space above the garage serves as playroom, craft/hobby room, or a guest-room and is accessible from both upper floor and garage level.

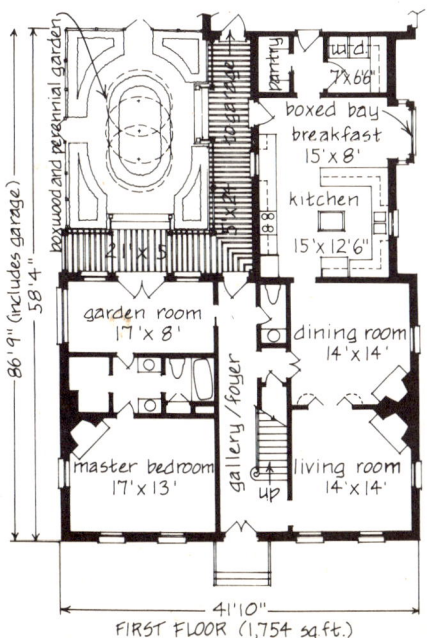

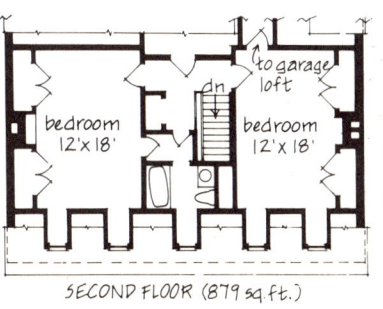

1123

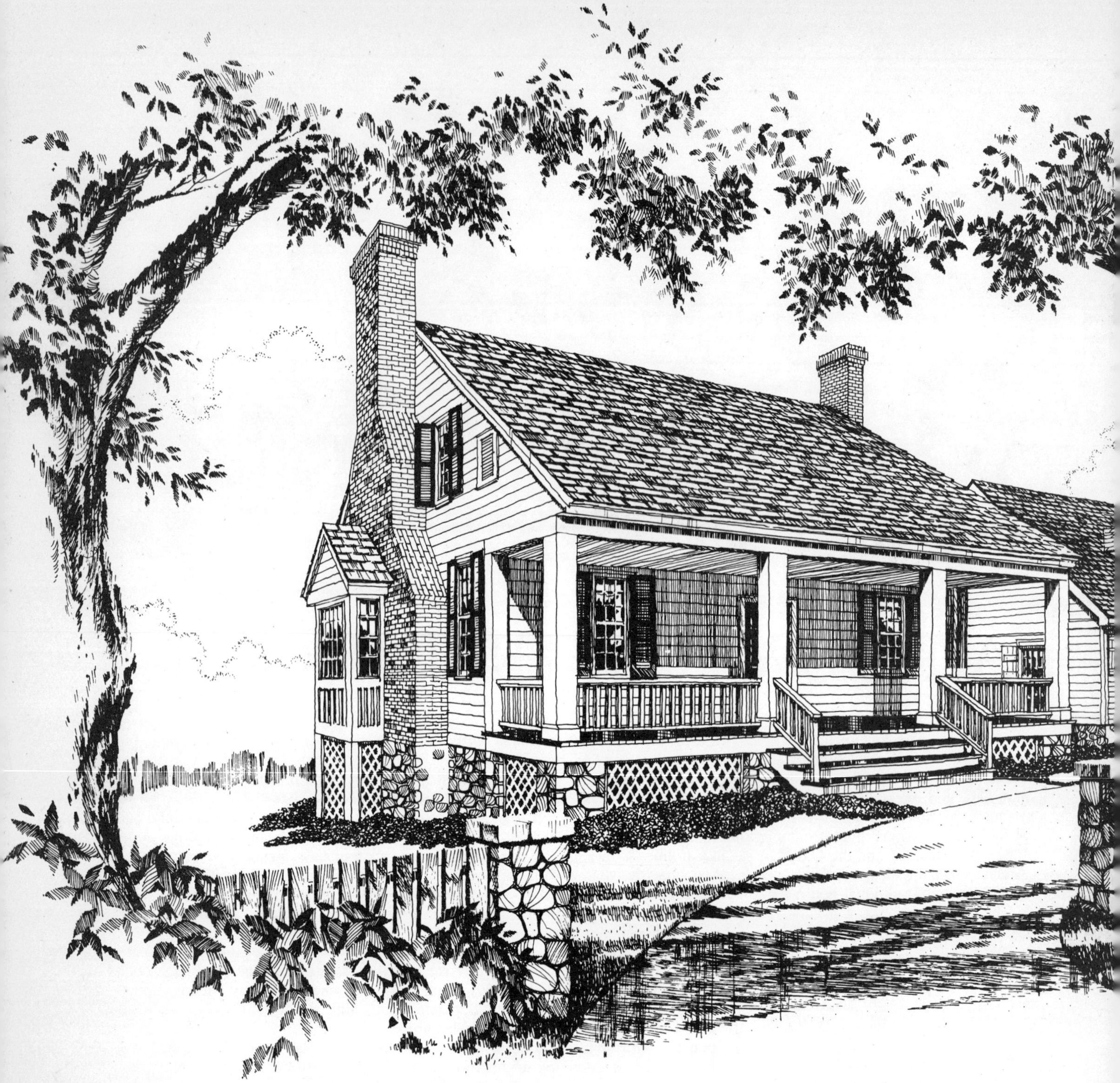

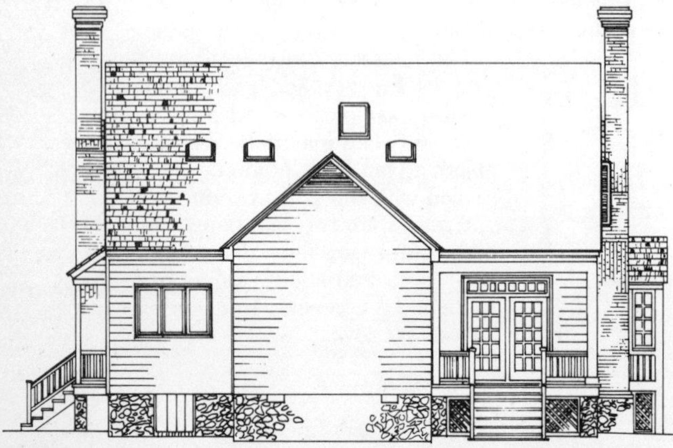

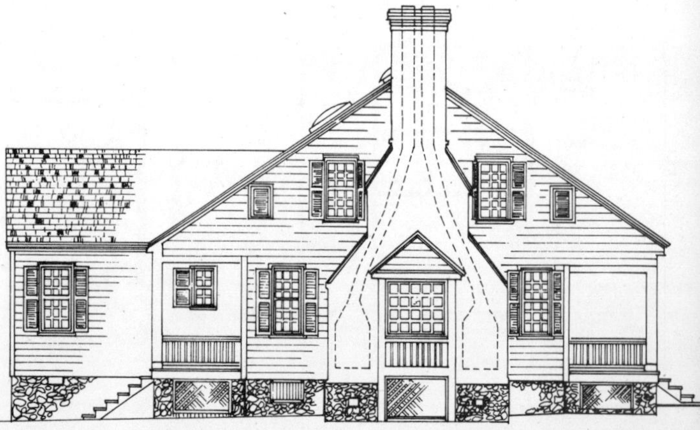

SLOOP POINT FARMHOUSE

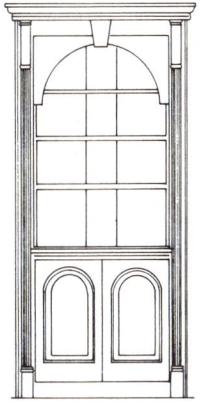

Some of the most appealing Southern houses are just one step removed from dogtrots or log cabins—frame farmhouses noted for their simplicity, sturdiness, and comfort. Modeled after Sloop Point Plantation, one of the oldest frame houses in North Carolina, our house retains the character of a centuries-old farmstead.

Square wooden pillars support a broad welcoming porch, which shades the house from summer sun. Entry is through a broad center hall flanked by living and dining rooms. A large family room with beamed ceiling, oak floor, and stone fireplace forms the heart of the first-floor plan; it opens to a comfortable sitting porch at the rear. There is also a downstairs bedroom for owners or guests.

An interesting feature of the original house, which has been retained in the new plan, is the small sunroom set into the chimney wall off the living room. With a brick floor and window walls above a simple wainscot, it shares warmth from the flanking fireplaces and could serve either as a small garden room or snug sitting nook for winter afternoons.

Upstairs, there are three large bedrooms, two baths, and a practical laundry room with space for sorting, folding, and ironing. Optionally, this area could become a sewing room or workspace, with a laundry located in the breakfast room beneath the stairs.

The house has about 2,600 square feet of heated space with more than 400 additional square feet in porches. A garage plan with a loft is included with the regular floor plan.

Weathered wood siding, a wood-shingle roof, and handmade bricks of local red clay contributed to the primitive, deep-country look of the original dwelling, and that look has been re-created in our contemporary version. Foundations, once a blend of rounded ballast stones from ships' holds, mixed with beach stones and coral, have become irregular stone with lattice panels between.

Originally built in 1730 on Topsail Sound, Sloop Point faced the Intracoastal Waterway and served as the main house for a small plantation growing mulberries for silk production. This new version was designed by Raleigh designer Jay Cardy.

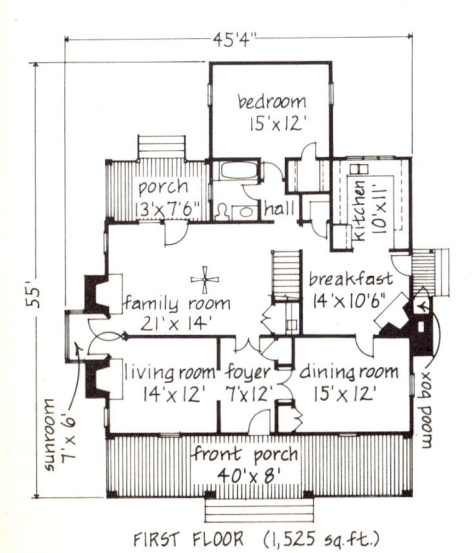

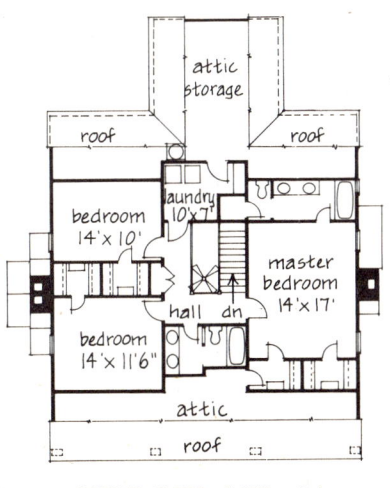

1120

FIRST FLOOR (1,525 sq. ft.)

SECOND FLOOR (1,075 sq. ft.)

COME HOME TO A CLASSIC

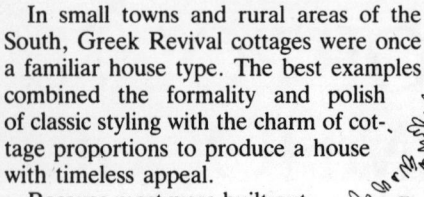

In small towns and rural areas of the South, Greek Revival cottages were once a familiar house type. The best examples combined the formality and polish of classic styling with the charm of cottage proportions to produce a house with timeless appeal.

Because most were built outside of the South's large cities, they were often owner (or carpenter) designed and built. And although often similar in size and form, they became charmingly individual with the owner's selection of architectural details.

Our Classic Cottage was inspired by the earlier, 19th-century homes. Designed for *Southern Living* by Architect Bill Phillips, AIA, of Mobile, it would be comfortably at home in town or in the suburbs.

Simplicity and symmetry help to create the cottage's classic good looks. Outside, a low hipped roof projects from the main body of the house to form a simple portico. Six slender columns support the porch roof and are set at angles into the porch floor. Crisp carpenter lace in the form of brackets at porch columns add turn-of-the-century appeal. Dressing the foundation are latticework panels set between redbrick piers.

The front gallery is as carefully detailed as an interior room. Flush siding on the gallery wall accentuates classic architectural trim. Floor-length windows are shuttered and are set within fluted casings. Fluted moldings also surround the paneled front door and flanking sidelights, and the doorway is topped by a transom.

Inside, a center hall foyer separates formal living and dining rooms. Cased openings replace doors off the foyer, providing easy access between rooms and opening the rooms visually in the process. For purposes of elegance and coolness, ceilings on the main floor are raised to 10 feet. Interior walls are dressed with base, crown, and accessory moldings.

Separating the dining room and kitchen is a small room that serves as a butler's pantry. To the rear of the plan, an all-purpose sunroom features a fireplace and window walls.

The master bedroom, dressing room, and bath are on the main floor. Upstairs are two spacious bedrooms with double closets and a shared bath.

1121

FIRST FLOOR — 2,375 sq.ft. (heated) / 246 sq.ft. (unheated)

SECOND FLOOR

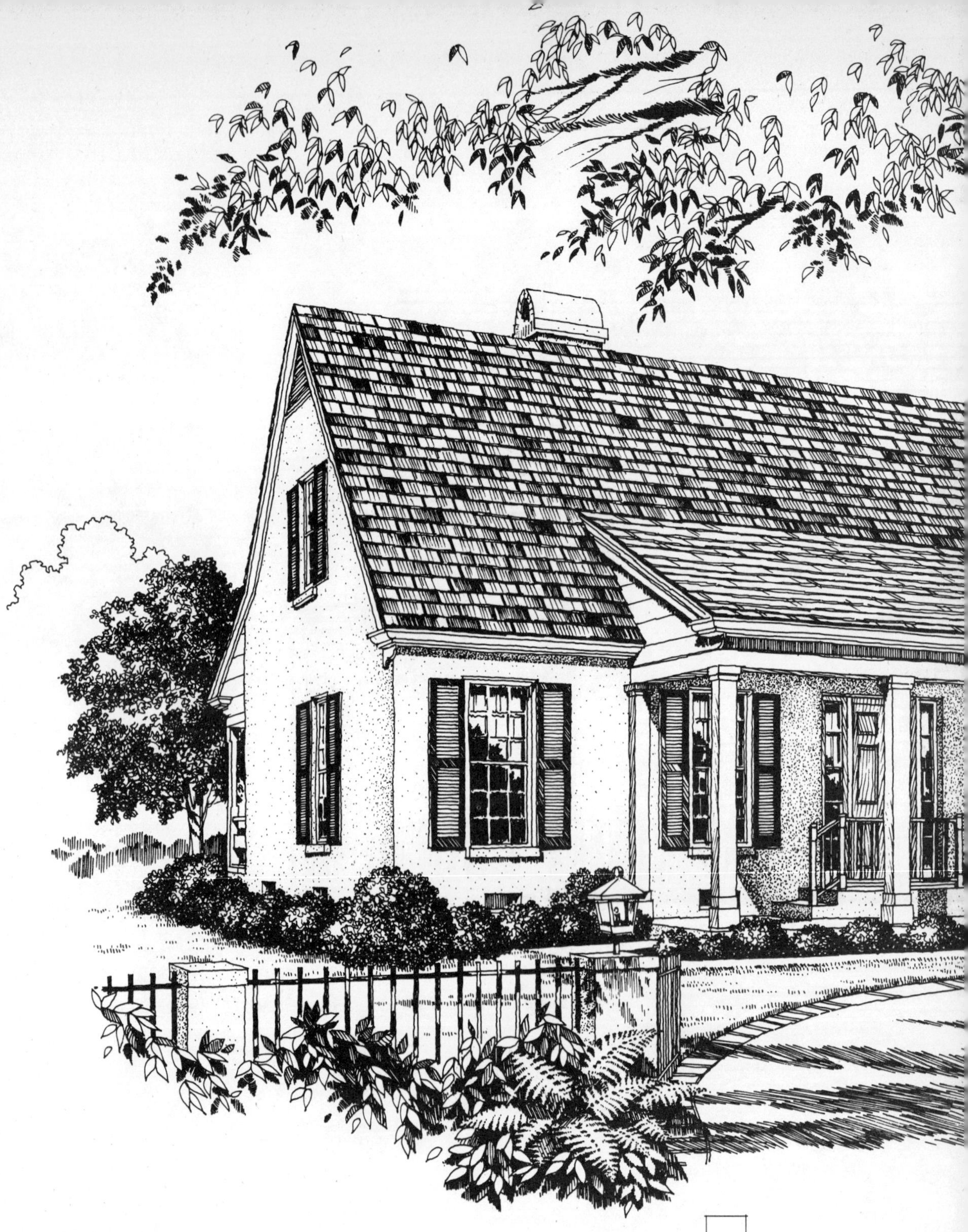

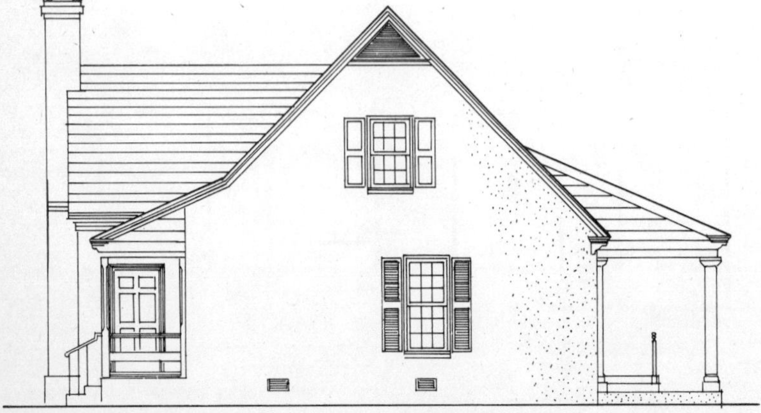

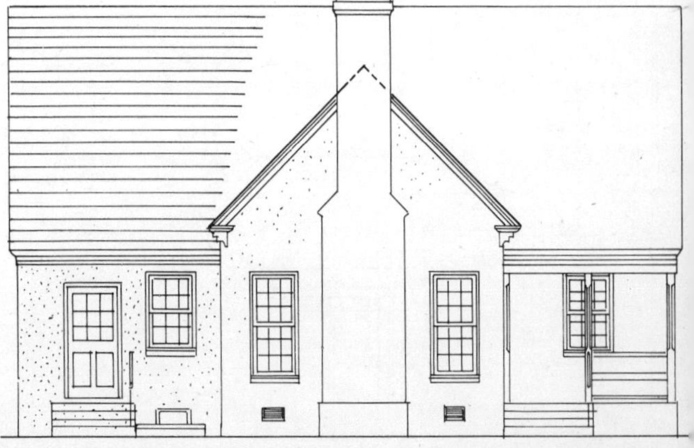

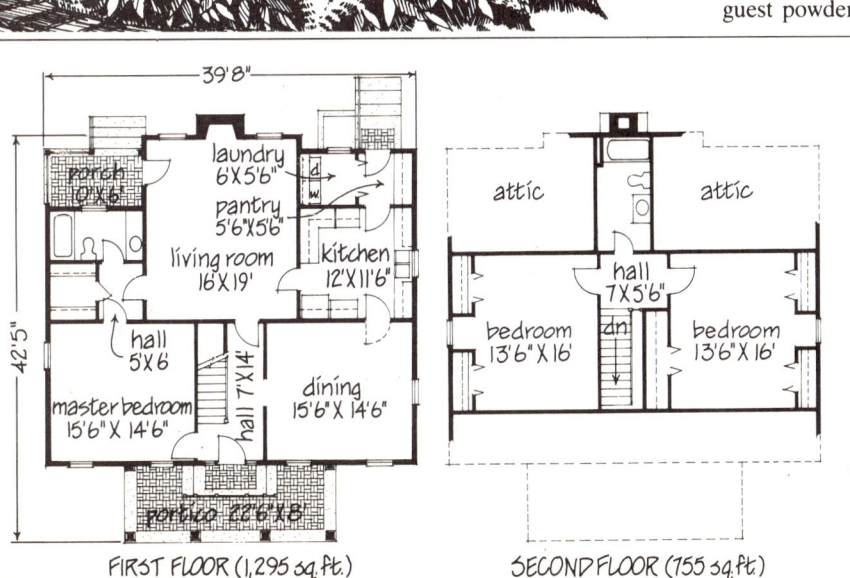

DETAILS MAKE THE DIFFERENCE

Precise proportioning and thoughtful detailing can make a small house special and distinctive. That's the case with our traditional stucco cottage, designed by Architect Frank McCall, Jr., AIA, of Moultrie, Georgia. An appealing blend of formal and farmhouse characteristics, it achieves the simple elegance usually associated with much larger homes.

The careful detailing starts outside. Stucco with wood trim gives a soft, finished look to the walls. A gabled roof is topped by a chimney of stuccoed brick with a graceful arched cap.

A columned portico with shed roof focuses attention on the entry. Beneath this portico, a smaller porch is recessed, raised, and dressed with a formal balustrade, which allows guests to enter from either left or right.

Details are even carried underfoot. Brick porch steps are laid in a basket-weave pattern with stucco risers and edging. Fluted trim surrounds the front door and sidelights, which have interior shutters for privacy by night and light during the day.

Inside, simplicity and comfort characterize the floor plan. A center-hall foyer leads to a spacious living room. A fireplace with brick hearth and stucco facing is centered between long windows in the rear wall. Adjacent to the living room and serving as its warm-weather extension is a small brick-floored sitting porch.

Separating the master bedroom and bath from the living room is a small hallway, which enables the bath to double as a guest powder room easily accessible from the living room.

In the right half of the plan are a dining room, which can handle formal or informal meals, and a roomy old-fashioned kitchen. Between kitchen and garden is a utility area, which combines the functions of laundry, pantry, and mudroom.

Two bedrooms, a stair hall, and bath occupy the upper story.

Compact overall dimensions of about 40 x 42 feet suit the house for a smaller lot. And its simplicity and use of standard sizes make the design affordable. The house has over 2,000 square feet of heated space, with about 250 square feet of unheated space.

1122

AN ALL-SEASONS HOUSE

Because of the extremes of climate found in many parts of the South, passive cooling is just as important to a homeowner as is passive solar heating. This house plan, suitable for weekend, vacation, or retirement use, offers a design that is truly adaptable from winter to summer. It can be effectively cooled by passive means for much of the warm season.

Since it is basically a house within a house, the design lends itself to staged construction. The basic living area at the center may be built first, with perimeter spaces added as time and budget permit. The perimeter spaces are used primarily as extensions of their adjoining rooms in summer, creating a screened living area at virtually every exposure of the house. In winter, heating loads are reduced by closing off the perimeter spaces, which then act as insulators for the house.

Its simple shape and use of natural materials give the house an appealing regional character. A metal roof adds to the vernacular feeling while reducing the cooling load by reflecting the summer sun. It may be painted or allowed to weather naturally. The house is designed to be built at least several feet above ground level over a ventilated crawl space. It can also be built on structural pilings in flood plains or coastal areas.

The basic plan is a 28- x 40-foot rectangle that contains the major interior spaces. An 8-foot perimeter area consists of porches and, on the south, prefabricated greenhouses, which act both as a home for plants and as solar collectors. There are about 1,300 square feet of heated space (excluding greenhouses), with almost 1,100 square feet in porches.

The hipped roof leads to a central cupola for ventilation in the summertime. All ceilings, with the exception of those in the bathrooms, are vaulted, creating the expansive effect of a lodge and, at the same time, channeling warmed air to the central cupola to be either exhausted or, in winter, recirculated.

The main floor contains two bedrooms and two baths, a spacious kitchen and dining area, and a large living room, which opens through glass sliders to a greenhouse on one side and an open trellised porch on the other. Additional sleeping space for guests could be gained in a roomy upper loft, accessible by a circular staircase and lit by roof windows. There is a large walk-in pantry and an airlock entry to prevent the escape of cooled (or heated) air.

The plan may be built with either full perimeter porches or with a combination of porch and greenhouse areas. An alternate plan, included with the working drawings, provides for two small children's bedrooms on the main floor with a playroom between. Also included is a site plan with planting ideas.

Because it successfully accommodates a full range of leisure activities—sunning, gardening, and relaxing—our all-seasons plan would make an ideal pre-retirement or retirement home. The designer is Mike Funderburk of Sunshelter, Raleigh.

1119

COURTYARD GARDEN HOUSE

Our Courtyard Garden House folds around a protected garden, which can be planted with evergreens and perennials for easy maintenance and year-round appeal. It's a true indoor/outdoor house with almost every room enjoying either a beautiful view of the garden court or direct access to it.

The courtyard garden and its enclosed gallery form the focal point for the design. The gallery acts as a transitional space between outdoors and in and is an ideal area for displaying artwork or a favorite collection of plants. It also provides a convenient spillover area for guests when entertaining.

The compact U-shaped plan contains about 2,400 square feet and a formal arrangement not normally found in a house of this size. Traditional moldings, 10-foot-high ceilings, and carefully planned views between house and garden help accomplish this formality. Brick and tile flooring and good indirect light turn the interiors into a series of gardenlike rooms.

The plan is divided into three basic zones: private area, which includes master bedroom and bath; public area, which includes foyer, gallery, half-bath, living and dining rooms; and family area, which contains kitchen, breakfast/den, and two additional bedrooms and a bath.

Arches are used as elegant design accents both indoors and out. Arched openings in the foyer, gallery, and dining room repeat the shape of the brick arches on the porch arcade.

The living room features arched windows and a formal fireplace set between built-in cabinet bookcases. A small library off the living room is entered through a wide arched opening. With floor-to-ceiling bookcases and a window overlooking the side garden, the library offers a quiet sitting area for reading.

The garage is designed to complement the house and includes a porch, workshop, service yard, and garden storage area. If the garage is sited as indicated in our layout, it also defines the fourth boundary of the courtyard, thereby making it a true outdoor room with an atrium feeling.

Brick arches and dentils accent the formal house front, and corbeling at the eaves and chimney cap add formal, finishing details. The front porch is floored in herringbone brick and is open, but it could be glassed to become a garden room entry.

Our Courtyard Garden House was designed by Architect David Sullivan, AIA, of Phelps and Sullivan, Atlanta.

1127

A CLASSIC COUNTRY FARMHOUSE

Our classic farmhouse is simple and solid in the best country tradition, but formal detailing gives it an elegance that would make it equally at home in town.

A gambrel roof with flaring eaves lends a country flavor and also adds extra space to the upper floor. Brick wings flank the house's center portion, which is clapboard. (Stucco or stone might be substituted for brick depending on the area of the South where the house is being built.)

Deep porches front and rear shade the house; ceiling fans can be added to create pleasant outdoor living areas. The dormers feature casement windows topped by graceful fanlights. Long windows, latticework trim, and well-detailed columns complete the traditional farmhouse look.

The floor plan is simple but flexible. The house may be built with or without the master bedroom wing. If built without, the plan offers a three-bedroom, two-bath house of about 2,400 square feet. With the addition of the downstairs bedroom wing, the house becomes a four-bedroom, three-bath home of about 2,800 square feet.

Half of the upper floor may be left unfinished and then completed later as a playroom or upstairs sitting room.

One appealing part of the design is the informal, open-plan kitchen featuring a vaulted ceiling, island work area, glass-front cabinets, and an old-fashioned country cupboard. A skylit breakfast room overlooks the rear garden. A combination laundry/pantry makes the kitchen as efficient as it is pretty.

Like the kitchen wing, the master bedroom wing features a cathedral ceiling. A spacious adjoining bath includes a dressing room, walk-in closet, separate bathtub and shower, and a window seat with built-in linen storage.

The large room to the rear of the downstairs plan could serve as either a comfortable family great room or as a more formal living room.

To the left of the foyer is a separate dining room, and to the right is a room that could be used as either guest bedroom, nursery, or study. Stairs to the upper floor may be approached from either the kitchen or from the family room, giving even more flexibility to the plan.

Because of the extra headroom afforded by the gambrel roof, the upstairs is spacious. It includes two bedrooms and a bath, as well as the unfinished area.

The basement has a double garage and workshop. Construction drawings also provide details for an alternate crawl space foundation.

Our Classic Country Farmhouse was designed by Phillip Franks of Birmingham.

1125

FIRST FLOOR (1,836 sq. ft.)

SECOND FLOOR (960 sq. ft.)

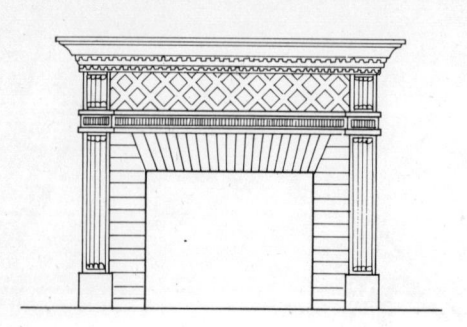

A HOUSE IN THREE PARTS

Inspired by historic homes in the Chesapeake area, our Maryland Tidewater House is made up of three distinct units—the main house, a central connector, and a master-bedroom wing. French doors set between square brick pillars convert the front portico into a hallway linking the three areas.

The main house contains formal living areas with side hall and powder room below and two bedrooms and a bath in the half story above. (A split heating and cooling system will allow this half story to be shut off for energy savings.) In the side hall, a fretwork balustrade dresses the staircase. Living and dining rooms have tray ceilings, which sculpture the space, adding a sense of elegance and volume.

At the center of the design is an open-plan connector, which includes family room, combination kitchen/breakfast room, pantry, and laundry. Brick flooring is used to tie these areas together visually. Skylights in the vaulted ceiling convert the connector into a bright, welcoming area with a garden feeling. The fireplace in the family room features a mantel with fretwork design adapted from drawings of a similar one at Snow Hill Manor in Maryland. A glassed porch to the front and an open garden porch to the rear give clear views to the outdoors.

The master-bedroom wing is the third element in the plan. Like the family room, it includes a vaulted ceiling, a formal fireplace with fretwork mantel, and built-in bookcases. A window seat located in the small vestibule linking the master bedroom with the rest of the house is a bonus feature. The master bath has separate dressing areas and a bathtub set into a bay.

In the architectural tradition of the Tidewater, exterior brick is laid in Flemish bond with alternating headers and stretchers. Steep-pitched rooflines and diaperwork detailing in the brick gable ends further reflect Tidewater influence.

There are about 2,400 square feet of heated space with almost 200 additional square feet in rear portico and porches. The house design was drawn by Architect Bill Phillips, AIA, of Mobile.

1126

2437 sq. ft. heated
192 sq. ft. rear portico and porches

First Floor — 68'6" × 30'8"

- hallway
- dining room 13' × 13'
- pantry 6' × 6'
- rear portico
- kitchen 8'6" × 9'
- family room 12'6" × 15'
- tub
- master bedroom 15' × 15'
- tray ceiling
- breakfast 8'6" × 6'
- living room 13' × 15'
- foyer
- front portico
- window seat

Main House | Connector | Wing

Second Floor
- bedroom 13' × 11'
- bedroom 13' × 10'
- dn

47

CARPENTER COTTAGE

Our Carpenter Cottage is crafted of good Southern wood—cypress, cedar, and pine. And it's artfully rustic, blending various elements of the woodworker's trade with the surprise of classic architectural features and a contemporary floor plan.

Carpenter elements outside include cypress board-and-batten walls, a cedar-shingled roof, and lattice accents. Traditional small-pane windows add to the house's cottage quality. Inside, carpenter detailing includes tongue-and-groove beaded-board ceilings and wainscots, exposed beams, and a roomy cedar closet on the second floor.

The basic design includes main house, connector, and wing and may be built in stages to suit budget or family size. For example, the house could be built as a 2,300-square-foot, three-bedroom, two-bath home. It could also be built with or without the latticed garden/sitting room. Or, with the addition of the bedroom wing, the house has the potential of becoming a four-bedroom, three-bath house of almost 2,900 square feet.

The plan is partially open, affording privacy to sleeping areas and a more contemporary design in living areas. The large, double-height living room has a fireplace, a balcony overlook, and steps down to a formal dining room. There's an open kitchen with breakfast area and a roomy butler's pantry, which offers extra storage for both kitchen and dining room.

The master bedroom has a cathedral ceiling with exposed beams and a quiet sitting area near the fireplace. Quarter-round windows flank the chimney and preserve privacy while bringing in additional light.

Two "indoor-outdoor" rooms—the latticed connector between main house and wing and the garden dining room—add to the plan's appeal. Although enclosed as part of the house's heated space, these rooms—with window walls, skylights, and views to the gazebo and arbor—are as much a part of the garden as of the house.

Two bedrooms, a bathroom, and a cedar closet share the upper floor, and there's the bonus of a gallery that overlooks the living room below.

A trellised arbor links house to garage. The garage has a loft that could be used as a workshop or artist's studio. The loft is lit by a large fan-topped window. The garage walls are overlaid with trellises, turning the area between house and garden into a private garden. A whimsical gazebo anchors the garden.

For a silver-gray finish on the cottage, the cypress may be treated with a bleaching oil or a transparent stain. Carpenter trim (the moldings, windows, trellises, and arbor) may be accented in either white or deep red.

Our construction drawings include details for a crawl space foundation and also include planting suggestions for a small garden off the kitchen.

Our Carpenter Cottage was designed by Architect David Sullivan, AIA, of Phelps and Sullivan, in Atlanta, Georgia.

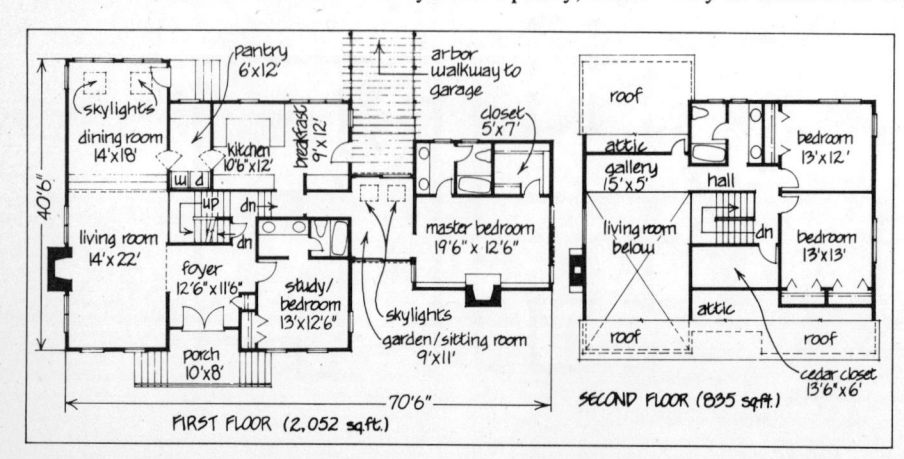

1124

A RUSTIC FARMHOUSE

Our rustic stone and cedar farmhouse is as comfortable and sturdy as the country original that inspired it. And along with its old-fashioned appeal comes the bonus of practicality: Its two-story design has a compact foundation and roof, which allows more square footage for the money than a similar-size single story or story-and-a-half design.

Stacked stone and board-and-batten cedar siding create its natural good looks. (Brick or stucco may be substituted for stone, if desired.) Angled bay windows and a whimsical spoke window beneath the peak of the gable add a country flavor. Porches, complete with old-fashioned swings, stretch living space by creating extra warm-season living rooms.

Rooms are large and simply laid out. On both main and upper floors, they are arranged around the central staircase. Downstairs, they create a circular flow from the large family-style living room, through breakfast room and kitchen, and into the dining room. Upstairs, the staircase serves as a divider between the master bedroom and the other bedrooms.

The kitchen is galley type, with a practical pantry and utility/mudroom to the rear. The bright bay-windowed breakfast room is for family meals, and there's a separate dining room for the more formal occasions. Country-style tongue-and-groove wood wainscots in the dining room, hall, and breakfast room underscore the farmhouse's casual country mood. With its paneling and rugged stone fireplace, the living room can be either formal or country.

The master bedroom features a tray ceiling, a fireplace, and easy access to the upstairs sitting porch. The adjoining bath has a large dressing area and walk-in closet. Across the stair hall, two roomy bedrooms share a bath.

The optional basement-level plan contains a workshop and single-car garage, as well as a large room that could be used as either a playroom or office.

Our Rustic Farmhouse plan was designed by Phillip Franks of Birmingham. The 3-bedroom, 2½-bath plan offers about 2,500 square feet of heated space, excluding the basement level.

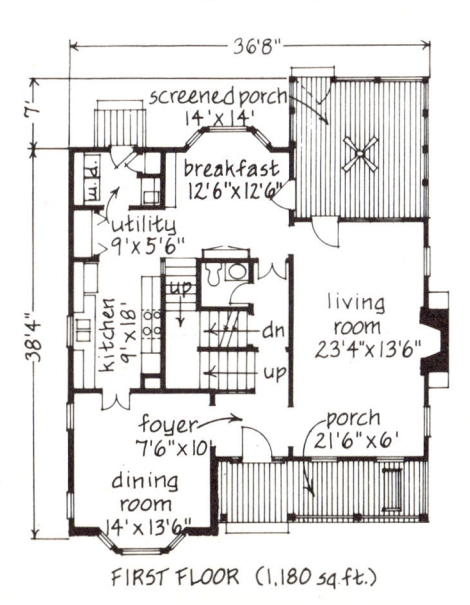

1129

FIRST FLOOR (1,180 sq. ft.)

SECOND FLOOR (1,268 sq. ft.)

GALLERIES COOL OUR GULF COAST COTTAGE

A curving balustrade leads guests up to the shady galleries of our Gulf Coast Cottage. Raised high on brick piers to keep its owners cool and dry, this cottage is an attractive reminder of the traditional Low Country homes of the South.

A high hipped roof covers galleries on three sides of the house. These galleries are broad and deep, forming a functional "cool zone" around the front of the house and working with transomed double doors to help ventilate the house naturally. Special millwork and trim add crisp definition to the simple, basic lines of the house.

The plan includes 3 bedrooms and 2½ baths in approximately 2,500 square feet of heated space. It offers the formality typical of older Southern homes and a semi-open floor plan often associated with today's houses.

For example, the living room, center hall, and dining room may be used separately or as one large room for entertaining. Wide cased openings create one spacious sweep of space, while perimeter galleries afford spillover space for summer parties. Ceiling heights are 10 feet throughout the house.

Both the family room and the master bedroom are roomy and comfortable. Outside each, a sun deck steps down to an enclosed courtyard with a garden pool. A latticed wall provides a privacy screen but admits cooling breezes.

A service pantry, with areas for storage and laundry, divides the kitchen and dining room.

Working plans for the cottage include a separate double garage with a similar look.

The design for our lovely Gulf Coast Cottage is by Architect Bill Phillips, AIA, of Mobile.

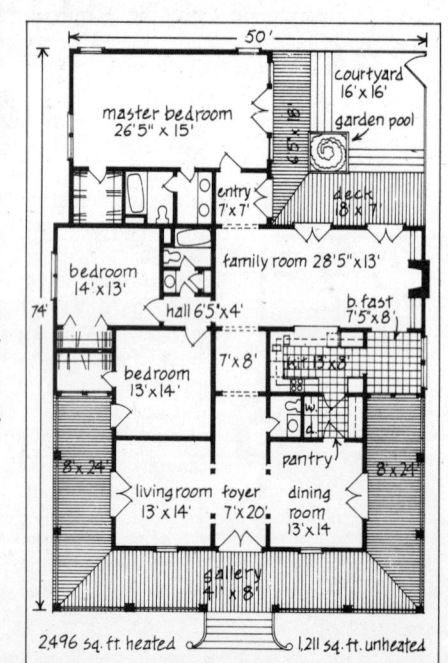

1131

51

SMALL HOUSE WITH APPEAL

With trellised gazebo entry and rear viewing deck, our basic two-bedroom plan has the appeal of a vacation house. It also offers the practicality of a first-time or retirement home. With compact overall dimensions, it is designed to fit comfortably on a small lot, whether urban, suburban, or beachfront.

Its small size (approximately 1,400 square feet heated) and simple detailing make the house relatively economical to build. The plan includes some special design features that give it the feeling of a much larger home.

For example, a vaulted ceiling and a full window wall in the living-dining area add volume and open the rooms to the outdoors. An adjacent deck provides additional fair-weather living space.

A fireplace adds winter warmth, while operable skylights combine with breeze-catching casements and ceiling fans to ventilate the house during the summer months.

The plan offers unusual flexibility for a house so small. The entry hall doubles as a gallery space and allows access to all major downstairs rooms. The master bedroom may be located downstairs for convenience or up in the skylit loft, which has an overlook into the living area.

Flexibility in siting is another bonus. In warmer climates, a north orientation of the glass gable wall would provide good natural light and ventilation without significant heat gain. The window wall may also be sited for the lot's best view or toward the south for passive solar gain. If sited toward the street, a privacy screen wall could be added. To avoid excessive heat gain in the summer, the glass wall should not be faced west.

Our two-bedroom house plan was designed by Architect David Wagner, AIA, of Charlotte.

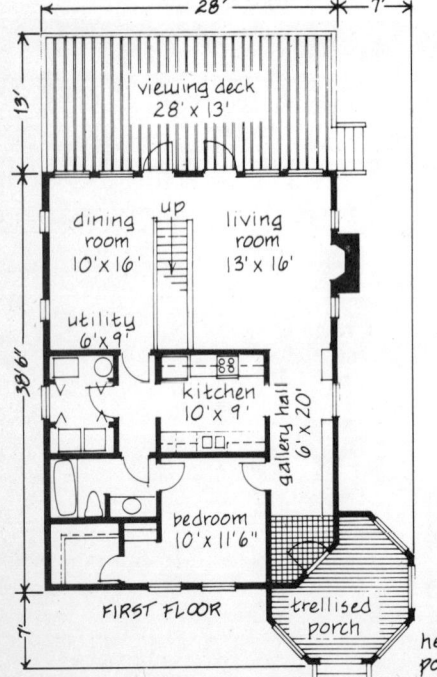

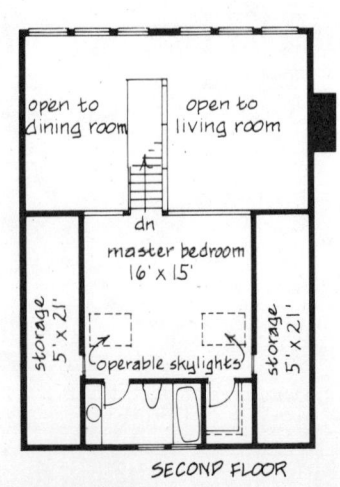

1132

FLORIDA GARDEN HOUSE

A privacy wall wraps our Florida Garden House, creating a welcoming entry courtyard. Although the front courtyard is only 13 feet deep, there is room for planting beds and a small pool filled with fish.

This house was originally built as a *Southern Living* Idea House, and it was the first one built in Florida. Its design reflects the climate of the Lower South. An open plan, floor-to-ceiling windows, overhanging roof, and cross-ventilation will definitely help make it cool and comfortable if it's constructed in the Upper South or Southwest.

Inside the entry courtyard, the floor-to-ceiling glass front wall of the house reveals the open, inviting interior. The house is basically rectangular and measures 40 x 63 feet. Five-foot roof overhangs across the front and back shelter the glass walls from the sun.

The entrance gallery extends across much of the front of the house, linking the living and dining areas as well as providing a circulation path to the bedrooms at either end of the house. The ceiling in the gallery, and throughout most of the house, is the standard 8 feet. But in the living room, the ceiling soars to 16 feet. This raised ceiling helps define the seating area and also makes the house seem bigger than its 2,100 square feet.

The master bedroom, with a large walk-in closet and master bath, is located at one end of the house. The two children's bedrooms and their shared bath are at the other end.

Our Florida Garden House was designed by Architect Dean Winesett, AIA, Hilton Head Island, South Carolina.

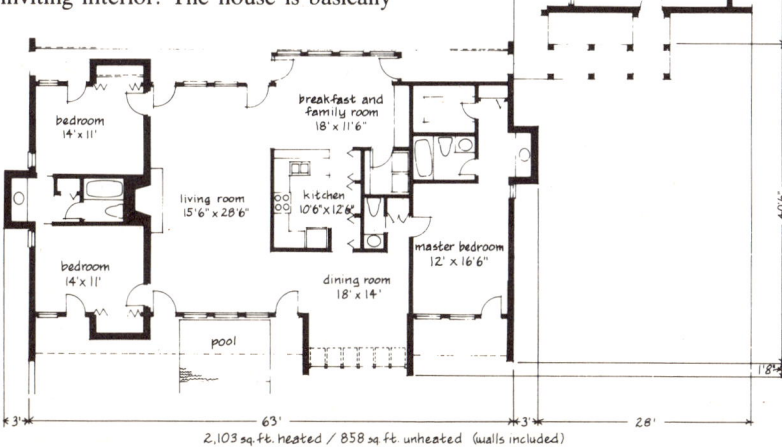

1133

A CLASSIC IN TWO SIZES

Some of the South's prettiest homes were built along the rivers and bayous of Louisiana. In most cases, they were also practical homes, built with as much regard for comfort as for good looks.

Our own Classic in Two Sizes home continues this tradition. A flexible floor plan allows it to be built at two different square footages; for convenience, the plan has been adapted for one story. The smaller version (shown here) is suitable for a 100-foot-wide lot. It includes 3 bedrooms and 2½ baths in about 2,600 square feet of heated space. By expanding the kitchen/breakfast area and master bedroom wings, the plan may be enlarged to include about 2,900 square feet.

For the larger version, setback requirements may indicate the need for a larger lot.

An appealing blend of classic and Creole influences, the house features light-colored stucco walls (brick may be used), a high hipped roof, and a deep U-shaped gallery at the front.

French doors and long casements work with covered galleries to cool and ventilate the house. Both windows and doors are fan topped in the classic style, and those opening to the front gallery are flanked by graceful quarter-round shutters. A balustrade atop the central portion of the roof borders an oversize skylight that brings light into the core of the house.

A center hall foyer features freestanding columns that divide the formal living and dining rooms. A cross hall leads to the master bedroom and kitchen wings at opposite ends of the plan.

Ten-foot ceilings throughout and tray ceilings in the master bedroom, living room, and dining room add volume and elegance. A separate breakfast area, walk-in laundry, and walk-in service pantry are features of both plans.

Our construction drawings give details for both versions of our Classic in Two Sizes home. They also include details for a small latticed summerhouse and a garage.

Architect Bill Phillips, AIA, of Mobile contributed the design.

1134

COUNTRY FARMHOUSE

With porches for shade and sun-catching decks, our Country Farmhouse plan captures what a good Southern house is all about—comfort.

One-story wings flanking the house's center section and porches with old-fashioned carpenter trim lend a rambling country flavor. At the same time, overall dimensions are relatively compact (59 x 41 feet), ensuring construction cost efficiency. The total plan contains 3 bedrooms and 3½ baths in approximately 2,400 square feet of heated space. Porches and decks add more than 600 square feet of living area.

An off-center entry breaks the symmetry of the plan to allow the most practical use of interior space. The center section of the plan contains a large kitchen/breakfast area and dining room with traffic flow around the staircase.

For convenience and privacy, the master bedroom with bath occupies its own wing on the main floor. The other wing has a living room with fireplace, a mudroom, and back entry.

Twin sun decks extend the living area in the wings, one serving as a pleasant extension of the family living area and the other as a private outdoor sitting area for the master bedroom.

The practical utility area combines the functions of an old-fashioned mudroom and laundry and provides extra space for a freezer and large utility sink.

Two additional bedrooms, each with its own bath and one with access to the upper porch, occupy the second story.

Ceiling heights are 9 feet on the first floor and a conventional 8 feet on the upper floor.

Our version is of molded brick with beaded-wood clapboard wings, but a more rustic look may be achieved by using board-and-batten wood siding at the center and stacked stone on the wings. Porches shade the front of the house from afternoon sunlight. A west orientation will therefore save on summer cooling costs and also let morning rooms (kitchen, breakfast room, and master bedroom sun deck) enjoy sunshine early in the day.

To suit budget and family size, this house may also be built in stages. Initially, a two-bedroom plan offers master bedroom and nursery or child's bedroom upstairs, with kitchen, breakfast, and living area below. The master bedroom and living room wings may be added later.

The Country Farmhouse was designed by Phillip Franks of Birmingham.

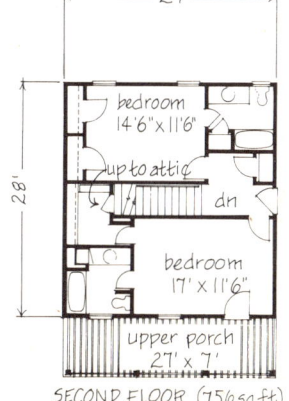

1135

TRADITIONAL WILLIAMSBURG

This Tidewater house plan offers all the trimmings—an assortment of traditional Williamsburg features plus the comforts and hospitality of home.

Modeled after Pembroke, a Virginia home built in 1701, our updated version retains the distinctive exterior detailing and unusual U-shaped floor plan of the original.

The house, with its adjoining court and terraces, forms a self-contained compound. The entry court, planted with boxwoods, leads guests to a raised brick terrace bordered by a Chippendale balustrade. Double doors are set beneath a narrow ribbon transom.

Inside, a formal foyer connects the three main sections of the downstairs—kitchen/service area, living areas, and master bedroom.

Living areas are spacious and comfortably formal. A traditional fireplace, centered in the back wall of the living room, serves as a focal point for both foyer and living room.

Pocket doors separate living, dining, and garden rooms, allowing them to be closed off, when desired, or opened to create one large room for entertaining. In addition, French doors open each of these rooms to the rear terrace for warm-weather parties.

The master bedroom occupies the plan's right wing. It opens through double doors to the garden room, whose corner position allows it to double as a sitting room.

The kitchen is roomy and features an island work area and separate breakfast room. The adjoining service area includes a walk-in laundry, pantry, powder room, and small potting room.

Twin stairs lead to the half-story above, which contains two additional bedrooms and a double bath.

The plan features 10-foot ceilings on the first floor and 8-foot ceilings on the upper level. Traditional base, crown, and accessory moldings are specified.

A covered walkway connects the house to a double garage with a skylit loft workshop. A Chippendale arbor softens the garden-facing garage wall.

This Traditional Williamsburg plan was designed by Architect Bill Phillips, AIA, of Mobile.

1136

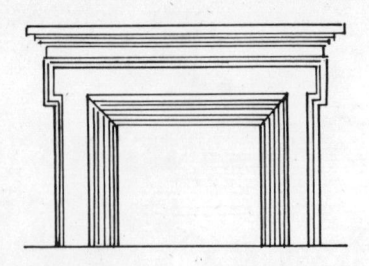

A HOUSE FOR COMFORT AND TRADITION

Simple but distinctive good looks and easygoing comfort are the hallmarks of the Tidewater style. This plan offers both in a design that provides for formal entertaining as well as informal family living.

The facade of the house's center section is brick laid in Flemish-bond pattern. Wings of equal proportions, but contrasting materials, flank the house, adding visual appeal. Rooflines are steeply pitched, with narrow gabled dormers typical of Williamsburg architecture.

The floor plan offers 3 bedrooms and 3½ baths in about 2,700 square feet of heated space. (The house may also be built without the two wings for a square footage of about 2,300.)

A center hall foyer separates formal living and dining rooms. The large breakfast room and bright garden room border the kitchen.

The plan offers the option of having the master bedroom downstairs with a large sitting room/library adjacent or having it in the larger bedroom upstairs. Then the downstairs room could be converted into a guest bedroom or study. Glass window walls enclose the garden room in the right wing. A fireplace makes it pleasant year-round, creating a natural gathering place for family and friends.

The upper story contains two bedrooms, each with its own bath, and a stair hall for storage closets.

A large screened porch links the house to an attached double garage with skylit studio, workshop, or playroom above. An open porch of simple detailing may also be added to the front of the house for a country look.

Ceiling heights are 10 feet throughout but can be vaulted in the library and garden room wings.

Our Tidewater plan was designed by Architect Bill Phillips, AIA, of Mobile.

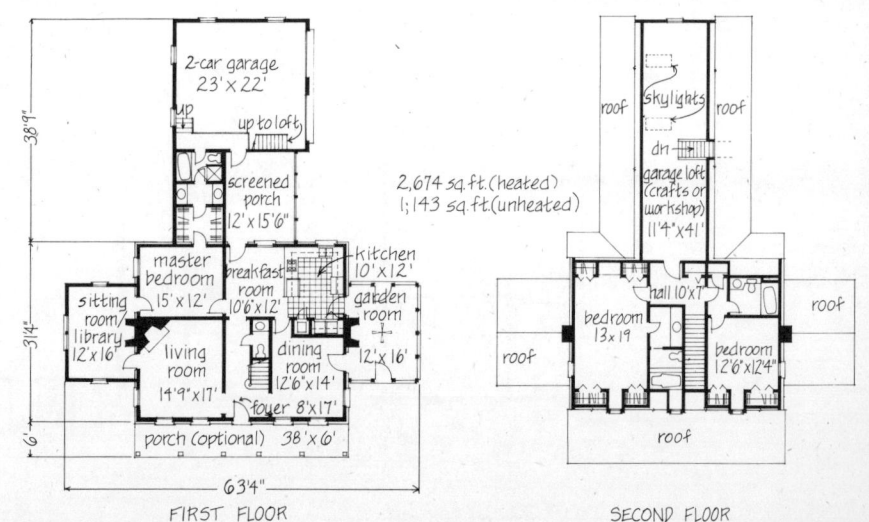

1137

OUR WILLIAMSBURG HOME

Dormers add a homey, traditional look to any house, and our Williamsburg plan has five. Slender and evenly spaced in the steep, gabled roof, they add the simple distinction that makes Tidewater architecture so appealing.

A graceful brick arcade dresses up the porch. House walls (except the front entry wall) are laid in the Flemish-bond pattern. Stucco or flush boarding on the front wall of the house contrasts with the brick porch and also sets off the trim surrounding the door and windows.

The chimney is an interior one. A distinctive cap covers the chimney stack, which notches into the roof that's below its peak.

Inside is a comfortable, flexible plan offering either 3 or 4 bedrooms and 2½ baths in almost 3,000 square feet of heated space. Among the special features of the plan are an open breakfast area and a formal dining room that includes a tray ceiling.

The downstairs master bedroom also has a tray ceiling; the room opens to its own sitting room with a corner fireplace. With its adjacent hall bath, the sitting room could also serve as guestroom or a nursery.

A skylit sun porch features long windows to the floor and could serve as a casual, summer family room.

A short connector, which contains the kitchen, a walk-in pantry, and a separate laundry/sewing room, links the house to its attached, double garage.

Upstairs are two more bedrooms, as well as a bath. Window seats with storage below are placed in each of the five dormers.

Our Williamsburg Home was designed by Architect Bill Phillips, AIA, of Mobile.

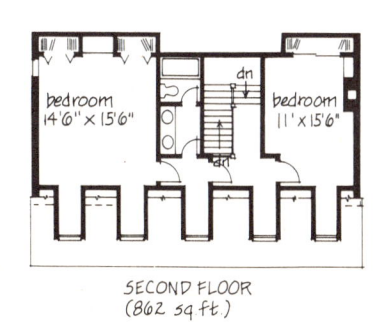

FIRST FLOOR (2,095 sq.ft.)

SECOND FLOOR (862 sq.ft.)

1138

59

STONE ACCENTS STUCCO IN OUR COURTYARD HOME

Our courtyard house comes with surprises and bonus features. Inside its traditional exterior is a gently contemporary plan. Outside, a series of private gardens and terraces expands living space and takes full advantage of a range of mild Southern climates.

Detailed in stucco with natural stone accents, the house is designed to be at home in either the coastal or piedmont South. Heated square footage for the main house is about 3,000, with over 800 additional square feet in courtyards and terrace. A bedroom or guest area can be added above the garage, which features its own fanlit dormer. (With foundation, framing, and roof already in place, the main cost of this expansion will already have been covered.)

Tall stone chimneys and gabled dormers create traditional "cottage" appeal. Inside, a semi-open plan features vaulted spaces and loft overlooks from the upper floor. High ceilings alternate with conventional 8-foot ceilings, making the house both dramatic and cozy.

The plan offers quiet and privacy to bedrooms while allowing activity areas, such as living and dining rooms, to share spaces. French doors in the master bedroom, living room, and at both ends of the foyer allow spillover onto surrounding courtyards and terraces.

The courtyard walls receive careful detailing. Constructed of stacked stone with naturally stained wood gates and panels, they offer privacy as well as convert lawn space into a low-maintenance outdoor living room.

Architect David Sullivan, AIA, of Phelps and Sullivan, Atlanta, contributed the design.

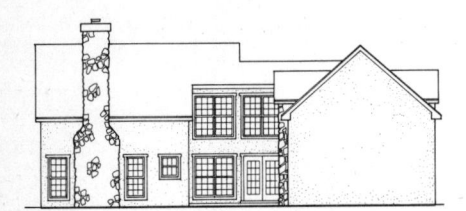

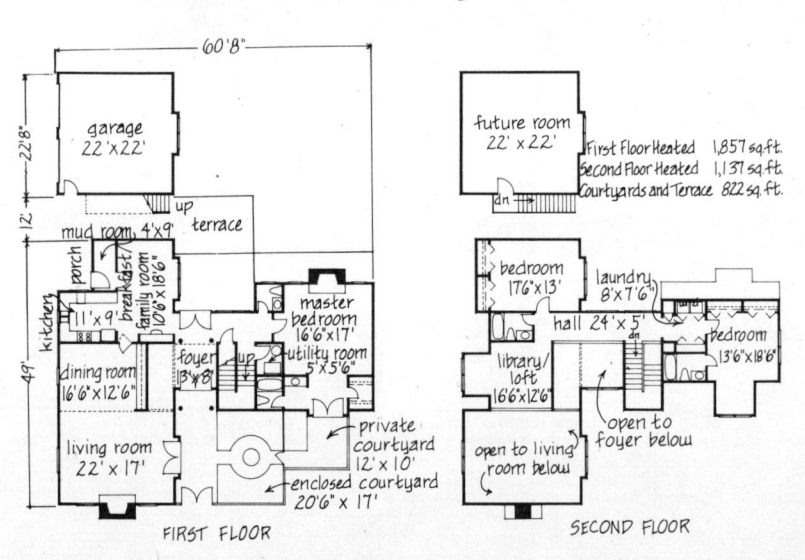

First Floor Heated 1,857 sq. ft.
Second Floor Heated 1,131 sq. ft.
Courtyards and Terrace 822 sq. ft.

1142

OUR VIRGINIA HOUSE

Adapted from the classically simple lines of the historic Wythe House located in Williamsburg, our two-story brick home offers generous servings of tradition and comfort. Precise proportioning and simple detailing give the design the distinctive flavor of Virginia.

A double-door entry set beneath the characteristic jack arch and ribbon transom welcomes guests inside. Brick is laid in Flemish-bond pattern with additional jack arches above the windows. A belt course separates the first and second levels, and a beveled brick water table defines the foundation.

Following the house's basic rectangular shape, interior rooms are simply proportioned but spacious. Each floor has almost 1,500 square feet of heated space, for a total heated square footage of about 3,000. The plan offers 2½ baths and the option of 3 or 4 bedrooms.

Living areas occupy the downstairs. Both the living room and the family room include traditional fireplaces. A spacious formal dining room features an adjoining service pantry. The open-plan kitchen includes a breakfast room large enough to handle most family meals comfortably.

Upstairs, a large master bedroom includes its own fireplace and a bath with double dressing areas.

Two additional bedrooms share a second upstairs bath. The study across the hall from the master bedrooom could serve as either a nursery or an additional bedroom for a child.

A walk-in laundry is functionally located to serve upstairs bedrooms and baths.

Ceiling heights are 10 feet on the first floor and 8 feet on the upper floor. Tray ceilings in the living and dining rooms and in the master bedroom add height.

This plan was designed by Architect Bill Phillips, AIA, of Mobile.

FIRST FLOOR (1,485 sq.ft.)

SECOND FLOOR (1,485 sq.ft.)

1139

62

PORCHES ADD POLISH

Porches front and rear add polish and attractive detailing to our Southern-style cottage. A diamond-work balustrade connects slender square columns, which in turn support a graceful, scalloped cornice. The diamond pattern is also repeated in the muntins of the fanlight.

Inside, a traditional floor plan offers about 2,550 square feet of heated space. A center hall foyer opens through graceful coved openings to formal living and dining rooms.

The kitchen and family room form the heart of the plan. The family room has an indoor-outdoor feeling. Its traditional fireplace makes it pleasant for fall and winter family gatherings; a window wall and adjacent porch orient it to the rear garden. Skylights over the family room also help to brighten the area.

Small wings enclose a breakfast room on one side of the family room/kitchen and a study on the other, each with a vaulted ceiling and its own fireplace. A practical butler's pantry for storing table linens and china is tucked between kitchen and dining room.

Wings extending from the back of the plan separate the master bedroom from the other bedrooms and enclose a courtyard. A long gallery connects the wings. Banked with windows, it opens to a deep, shaded sitting porch overlooking the garden court.

This plan was designed by Architect Bill Phillips, AIA, of Mobile.

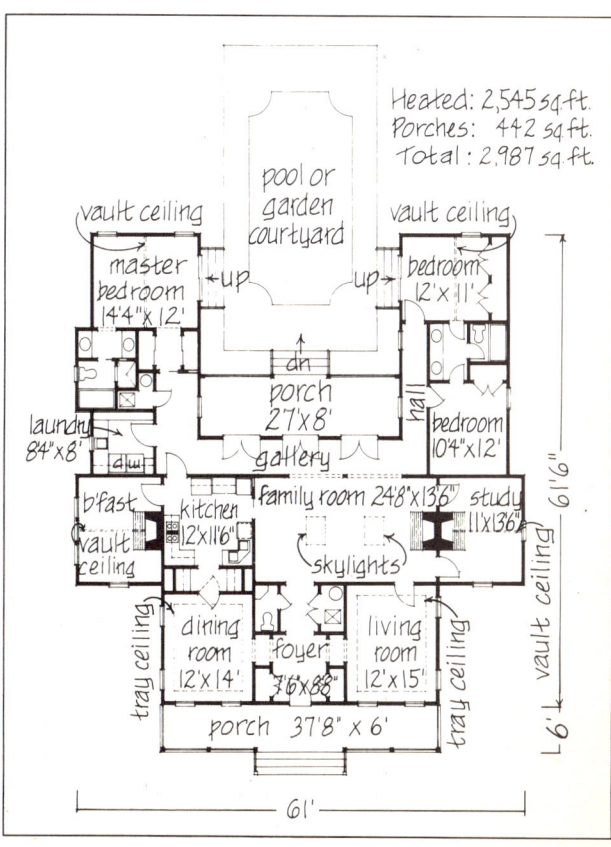

1143

Heated: 2,545 sq.ft.
Porches: 442 sq.ft.
Total: 2,987 sq.ft.

CHESAPEAKE COUNTRY HOME

Away from the larger towns of the Tidewater, housing styles were often simpler. Understatement was the basis for their appeal, as it is with our Chesapeake Country Home.

The exterior of the house is simply ornamented. Beaded-wood siding covers the house, with brick accents at the front porch, terrace, and chimney.

Special emphasis is given to the entry, with a wide, graceful fanlight covering the doorway. Carriage lamps and sidelights flank the double doors, and just above the entry, a circular vent accents a small gable.

Inside, an expansive hallway runs the depth of the house. At its end, a fanlit doorway, with detailing identical to the entry, opens to the rear terrace.

A combination living room/library includes a traditional fireplace and floor-to-ceiling bookshelves. French doors bordered by windows open the room to the terrace.

A large, open-plan kitchen includes a generous pantry and storage area and an adjoining skylit breakfast room. A separate work area provides space for cookbook storage and recipe reading. The dining room is formal with a tray ceiling and traditional moldings.

Bedrooms are placed in a separate wing. French doors and a vaulted ceiling open the master bedroom. Two additional bedrooms share a walk-through bath. The laundry is in a practical location in the hallway between bedrooms and breakfast room.

The one-story plan contains 3 bedrooms and 2½ baths in about 2,500 square feet of heated space.

Our Chesapeake Country Home was designed by Architect Bill Phillips, AIA, of Mobile.

1141

A FRENCH COUNTRY HOUSE

This plan recalls the rustic charm of an old French manor house. Board-and-batten cedar siding stained a soft gray, along with wood trim painted a deep red, lends a look of antiquity. The chimney is stuccoed with a curved tile cap.

A combination of high rooflines—pyramid, hipped, and gabled—gives the house its appealing mass, but more importantly, it allows for lofty, high-ceilinged rooms inside.

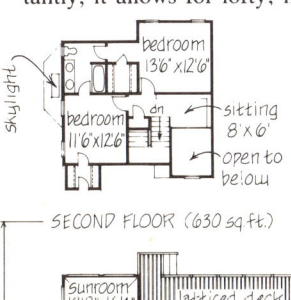

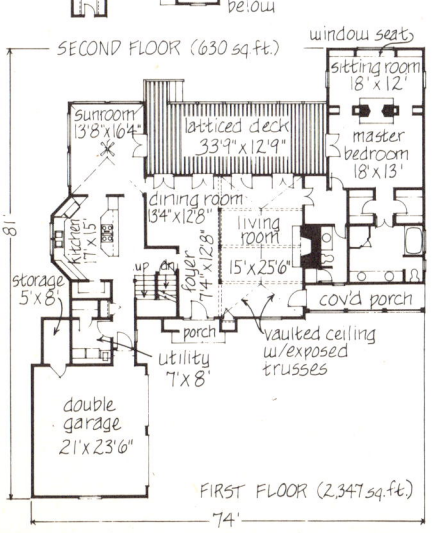

The plan offers 3 bedrooms and 2½ baths in approximately 3,000 square feet of living space. An optional plan for a basement details a fourth bedroom and bath as well as a workshop.

The front doorway is detailed with fanlight, sidelights, and traditional wood moldings. It is recessed slightly to provide protection from the weather. A fan window in the peak of the gable lights the double-height foyer as well as the upper-story landing.

The country style living room has a high, vaulted ceiling and exposed wood trusses. Lofty, but warmed by a fireplace that's slightly overscaled to fit the room's dimensions, it's a comfortable, informal room. A covered front porch, just outside, offers a dry storage area for firewood. Faced with lattice panels, it also screens the bedroom wing from the street.

The living room, dining room, and sunroom open through French doors to a protected deck. Open to the sky but enclosed by high latticed walls, it forms a "winter garden" that can be used for container-grown plants.

A bright and roomy kitchen includes both an island work center and a skylit bay area.

For convenience and privacy, the master bedroom is on the main floor. A small sitting room with fireplace, bookcases, and a fanlit window seat creates a cozy area away from the sleeping space. French doors also open the bedroom to the latticed deck outside. A small hall separates the master bedroom from the main living areas.

The living room, dining room, and foyer are separate rooms but are designed to function as a whole for parties.

Two bedrooms and a bath are upstairs. Built-in bookcases convert the upstairs hall into a small reading nook that overlooks the foyer.

The attached double garage is pulled forward to form a welcoming courtyard for guests. For owners, there is access to utility room, pantry, and kitchen through the garage.

Our French Country House was designed by Phillip Franks of Birmingham.

1146

LIVE THE COUNTRY LIFE

With three bedrooms and roughly 2,600 square feet, this plan has the rustic charm of a lakeshore lodge and the comfort of a home in town.

Materials and building components reflect the city/country mix. Walls of the wings are clad in board-and-batten silvery cypress, and the recessed front porch is faced with irregular, wood-mold brick. The fan-topped casement windows and a crisp, stickwork balustrade add in-town appeal to the front of the house.

The U-shaped plan falls naturally into zones, with the entry and living area at the center and kitchen/dining room and master bedroom in the flanking wings.

The half-story above contains two bedrooms, each with its own bath. An additional bedroom and bath are possible if the optional basement plan is used. (Our construction drawings include the basement plan.)

The plan's gallery-type foyer does triple duty. It serves as a welcoming point for guests, as a circulation corridor for the three areas downstairs, and as a small greenhouse.

Beyond the foyer, twin staircases rise to the floor above. Each enjoys an overlook into the foyer and great room below.

Skylights in the pitched ceiling flood the great room with natural light. Long, triple windows flank the fireplace, creating an open, window-wall effect.

A roomy kitchen includes an island work center and adjacent walk-in laundry. Pocket doors allow circulation from both the great room and dining room or the option of closing off the kitchen.

Both the dining room and master bedroom feature vaulted ceilings and fan-topped windows. The bedroom has two walk-in closets and generous dressing and bath areas.

Two back porches, one of which is screened, extend the living space.

This house was designed by Phillip Franks of Birmingham.

1144

OUR LOWLANDS HOUSE

The "raised-basement" house, with either 1½ or 2 stories above, was a distinct style along the coast and bayous of Louisiana. Because of the high water table in these areas, very few homes were built with below-ground basements.

Our Lowlands House continues this tradition and offers the option of building either with or without the raised basement.

Inspired by a small plantation house on Bayou Lafourche, our updated version retains the look of the Louisiana Lowlands. It's a usual coastal custom to use masonry at the raised-basement level, with wood clapboard above. Here, the basement level is covered in a molded brick. Broad galleries reinforce the regional look, shade the house, and serve as exterior hallways.

The raised-basement level includes a two-car garage, workshop or playroom, a large potting shed, and an optional guest-room or apartment with bath.

A graceful, double, exterior stairway leads to the main floor. Shuttered French doors open to a foyer, which separates living and dining rooms. The living room features a tray ceiling and a center fireplace flanked by built-in bookcases. The room can expand to 40 feet deep by including the galleries.

For convenience, the master bedroom is on the main floor. It includes a tray ceiling and a private balcony. The kitchen opens to a bright breakfast room.

The upper floor offers either three or four additional bedrooms. Two shared, compartmental baths are economical without compromising function. The heated and cooled area for the main and upper floors is 3,250 square feet. Porches and gallery add almost 600 square feet of living space.

Our Lowlands House was designed by Architect Bill Phillips, AIA, of Mobile.

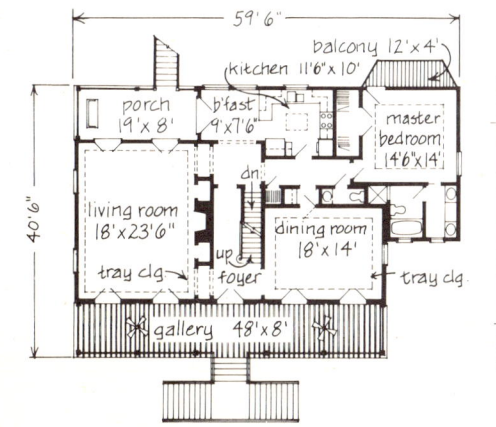

MAIN FLOOR (1,685 sq. ft.) 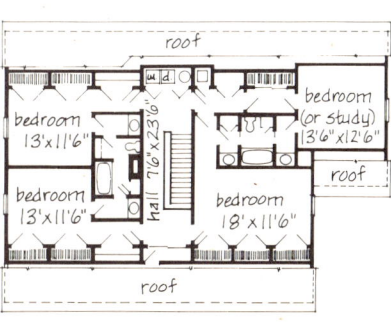   UPPER FLOOR (1,565 sq. ft.)

1149

TWO-FOR-ONE HOUSE

A simple but inventive way to combine privacy with sociability, this house plan features two homes in one.

The single-bedroom main house is one level with a semi-open plan. Designed as a comfortable apartment, it includes a spacious master suite with separate sleeping and sitting areas. A ceramic-tile floor, French doors, and a skylit ceiling brighten the garden room entry. Remaining spaces in the main house offer areas for cooking, entertaining, and indoor gardening.

Children or houseguests could be comfortably lodged in the second unit. Smaller than the main house but completely self-contained, it includes two bedrooms, bath, efficiency kitchen, and its own wraparound porch. A covered walkway connects the main house with the guesthouse.

The design offers a number of possibilities. The main house could be built first, with the second house added at a later date. In resort areas, or where zoning permits, the guesthouse might also be used for rental purposes. A fourth bedroom could be added by enclosing part of the porch on the guesthouse. Using the units as house and office or house and studio is another option. Or either unit may be built independently of the other.

Although our rendering and layout show a side-by-side relationship, the units may also be arranged front and rear to fit on a narrow lot.

Overall dimensions of the two units (with connector) are 129 x 84 feet in the side-by-side layout. If sited front and rear, dimensions are reversed. The bridge connecting the two may be shortened, if necessary. (Be sure to check lot dimensions and setback requirements to determine whether the design is appropriate for your lot.)

Both units are designed to be comfortable in warm, humid climates, with shade and natural ventilation. Florida Cracker styling includes cedar board-and-batten exterior walls, crawl space foundation, and a metal roof with deep overhangs.

There are roughly 2,000 square feet of living space in the main unit and almost 1,000 square feet in the second unit. Porches add approximately 2,500 square feet.

Our Two-for-One House was designed by Architect Ron Haase of Gainesville, Florida.

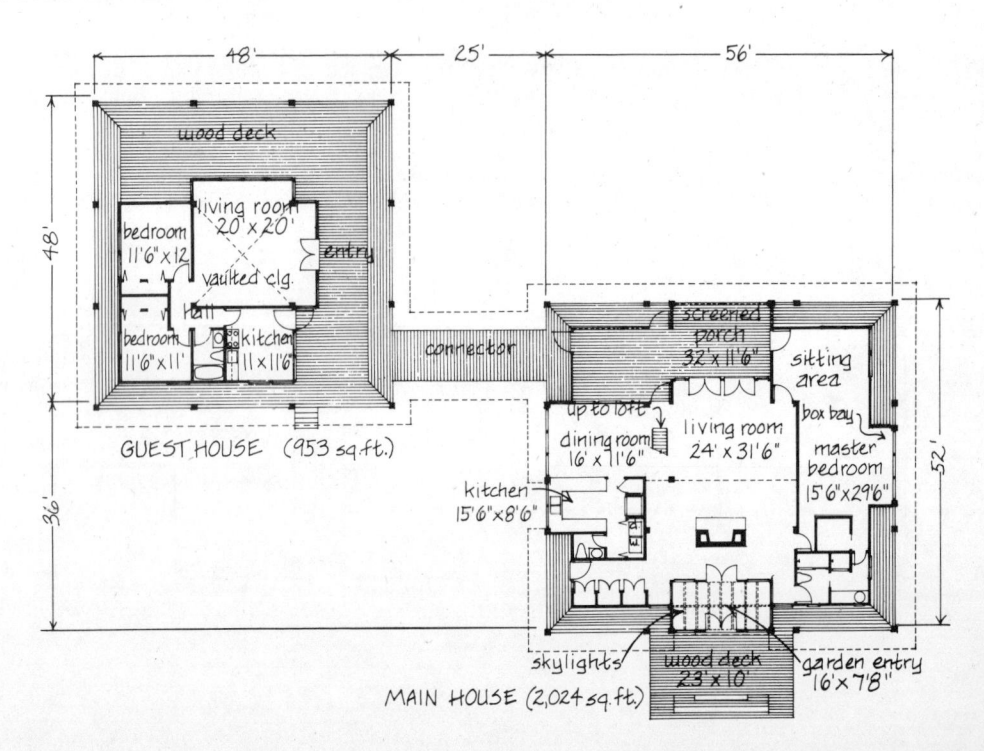

1148

CLASSIC VILLA

Its inspiration is classical, but clean lines and smooth finishes give our Classic Villa a contemporary feeling. Simple yet sophisticated, its one-level plan is comfortably elegant. It contains roughly 2,000 square feet of heated space.

The H-shaped, double-courtyard plan allows major rooms to open to light, fresh air, and garden views. In addition, both the entry and the rear arbor court offer spacious, fair-weather living areas.

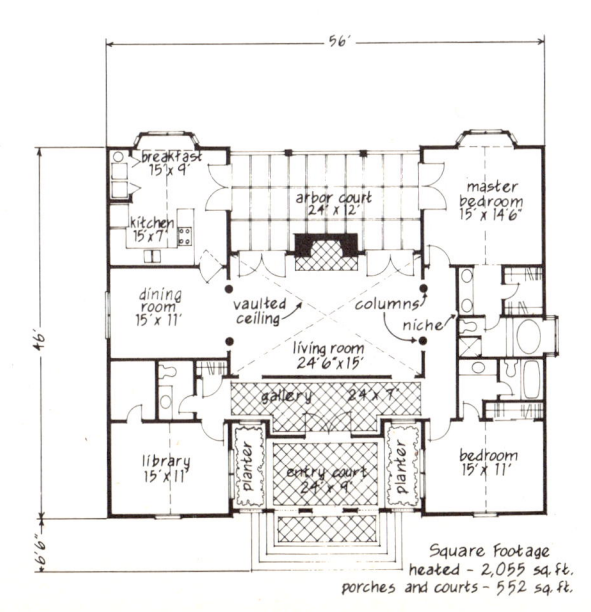

Exterior walls are of light-colored stucco with architectural trim in white. A pedimented wall with latticed windows screens the planted entry court from the street. The house is entered by stages, with raised terrace, entry court, and gallery welcoming guests inside.

The living room is at the center of the plan. Four freestanding columns underscore the room's classical look and frame views into the dining room and hallway. The hallway has a wall niche for spotlighting a favorite piece of art or family collection.

French doors in the living room flank a traditional fireplace and lead to the arbor court outside. Covered with a trellis, the court can be planted for dense shade or left open to catch patterned sunlight. Or, as another alternative, it can be glassed to create a solarium or garden room.

The library can be converted to either a third bedroom or a guestroom by expanding the powder room to a full bath. (A conversion plan is included with our working drawings.)

Ceilings are vaulted at the four corners of the plan and in the living room and are a conventional 8 feet in other areas. Plantation louvers dress interior doors and windows, emphasizing the simple, classic look. Suggested floor finishes include a combination of overscaled white ceramic tile and bleached hardwood. Crown, base, and accessory moldings are specified.

Our Classic Villa was designed by Architect David Sullivan, AIA, of Phelps and Sullivan, Atlanta.

1152

70

OUR PIEDMONT HOUSE

A steep, gabled roof shelters our Piedmont House, and a lean-to porch gives it a comfortable, rustic flavor. Local materials, stone and cedar, also add to the look.

Cottage details are carried inside with an easygoing, compact floor plan. A short, L-shaped hallway joins the three major areas of the downstairs plan. (The central staircase allows for minimal hallway space upstairs, too.)

The living room has the feeling of a country lodge, with stone fireplace and built-in bookcases. Pine paneling, which may be given a natural stain or painted white for a dressier country look, covers the walls. The dining room features an appealing box bay with floor-to-ceiling windows on three sides and recessed downlights, making it a focal point by day or night.

The family-style kitchen is roomy. Two sets of French doors into the sunroom allow a circular traffic flow and enable kitchen, breakfast room, and sunroom to work together as a casual activity center for the house. A wraparound deck stretches this family living area even more.

A series of small but special places adds to the plan's appeal. A skylit desk tucked into the hall across from the laundry serves as a compact home office. A private sun deck with lattice screening may be added off the master bedroom.

Although we show a 4-bedroom, 3½-bath design, the plan might be built initially as a 3-bedroom, 2½-bath house with the upstairs "bonus area" finished at a later date. If the bonus area is included, heated space is just over 2,800 square feet. If built as a 3-bedroom house, heated square footage is about 2,500.

Ceiling heights are 8 feet, with a vaulted ceiling in the sunroom and an optional tray ceiling in the master bedroom. Plans for an optional basement with two-car garage are included with the working drawings.

Our Piedmont House was designed by Phillip Franks of Birmingham.

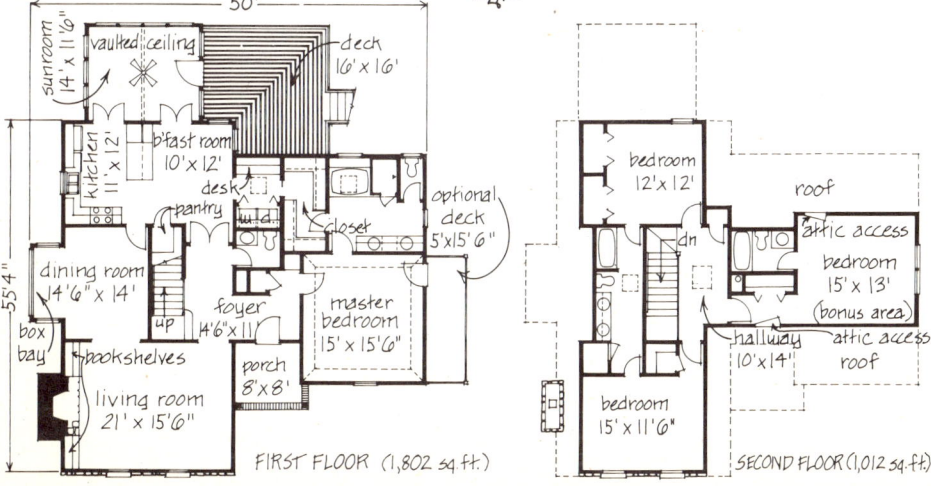

1151

NORTH FLORIDA COTTAGE

A good Southern house gives porches their fair share of the living space, and this house is no exception. It has three porches—one for privacy off the master bedroom, one at the front, and the other off the breakfast area. All three are cool and inviting through warm seasons.

Our example is based loosely on the Mary Perry house, built around 1880. The house is located near the Seville Square historic district in Pensacola, Florida.

Lacy latticework, scroll-saw porch brackets, and decorative cast-iron ventilators, based on early patterns, re-create the old-fashioned character of the original.

The plan is one level, with 3 bedrooms and 2½ baths in approximately 2,000 square feet of heated space. Despite its "cottage" character, it contains many features found in much larger homes.

Bedrooms are at opposite ends of the plan, with family living areas in between. The master bedroom is large and has a private sitting porch screened by airy lattice panels. A central kitchen includes a pantry and opens to a breakfast area brightened by two skylights.

The formal dining room has a separate service pantry for storing china and table linens. Ten-foot-high ceilings and long, breeze-catching windows add elegance as well as comfort.

Our North Florida Cottage was designed by Architect Bill Phillips, AIA, of Mobile.

1150

KENNESAW COUNTRY HOUSE

Exterior materials—fieldstone, wood siding, and stucco—combine to give our Kennesaw Country House an upland-country feeling. The dormer windows, gently scalloped porch arcade, and steeply pitched roof add to the country house look. This mix of elements also helps give the exterior a cozy, cottagelike appearance that belies its over 2,700 square feet of space inside plus bonus area.

The house is a basic 1½ story, with a gabled wing extending forward. This wing, which forms the great room, is done in stucco. Casement windows, fitted with transoms, flank the chimney that is centered on this wing. Stone steps lead up to a wide front porch, also bordered in stone. Square wood columns support three shallow arches across the front of the porch roof.

Inside, a central foyer runs through to the rear of the house. Cased openings near the front door lead to the great room on the left and the study/guest bedroom at the right. A full bath, located behind the study, doubles as a powder room. The great room, which measures about 19 x 18 square feet, has a 20-foot ceiling. Extensive use of stock trim for molding, the mantel, and built-in bookshelves gives the room a rich look.

A cased opening links the great room with the dining room. Another cased opening connects the great room with the breakfast room and kitchen. The kitchen features an L-shaped work counter and an additional work surface on the opposite wall. A two-car garage is just beyond the laundry room. A back stairway provides access to the bonus room above the garage.

Upstairs, the master bedroom is on one side of the main stairs. The master bath and dressing areas are fitted into the front dormers, creating an interesting series of spaces. The other two bedrooms share a bath.

For the design of the Kennesaw Country House, we worked with the firm of Design Traditions in Atlanta.

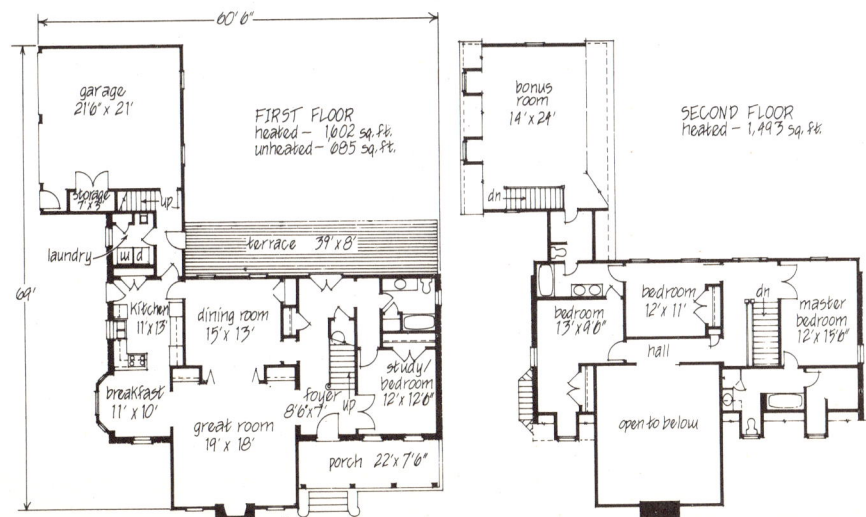

1154

Architectural rendering: Frederick Spitzmiller

74

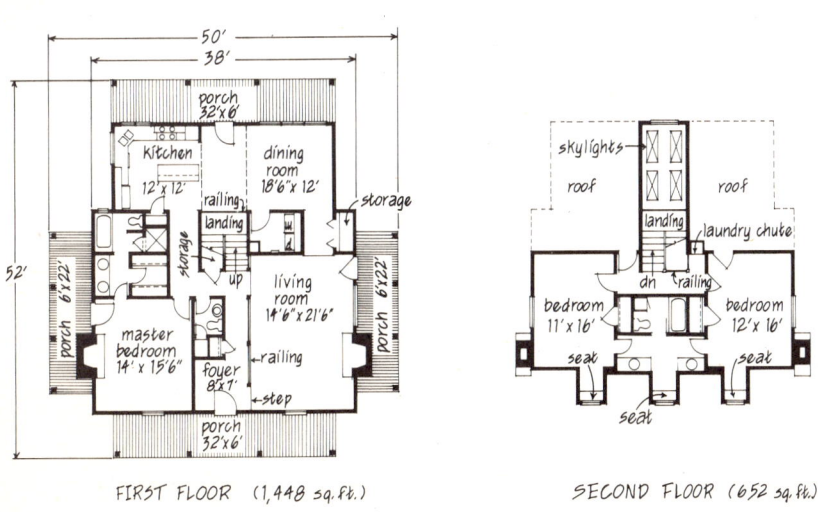

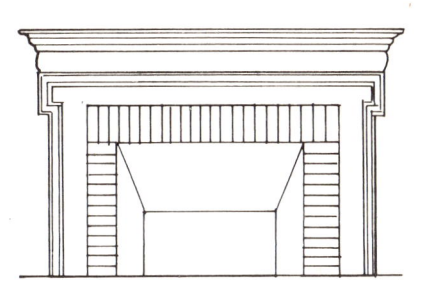

FOUR PORCHES HOUSE

Porches give this plan the look of a homestead set deep in the country. In fact, the design was inspired by just such a house, Chestnut Hill, built in the 1830s in West Tennessee. Lumber used in the original was taken from chestnut trees that were cut and seasoned on the site.

Twin chimneys and a steep, dormered roof retain the old-fashioned flavor of the original house. But the interiors are updated for comfortable living. The house has roughly 2,100 square feet of enclosed space. A semi-open floor plan and the use of high ceilings make it appear even larger.

For convenience and privacy, there's a downstairs master bedroom with its own fireplace and adjoining bath.

The kitchen is actually one large family gathering area. Flooded with natural light from a fan window high in the back wall and from four skylights in the vaulted ceiling, it's an airy, open room. The dining room does double duty, serving either as a cheerful family eating area or as a more formal "garden" dining room for guests.

Tucked between living and dining rooms is an alcove with storage for stereo, books, and games.

The upstairs plan includes some of the "cottage" elements that might well have been found in the original. There are three dormers, each with a window seat; a small landing overlooks the kitchen/family area.

The bedrooms share a convenient, pass-through bath with double dressing areas. A chute carries laundry to the utility room directly below.

Our Four Porches House was designed by Phillip Franks of Birmingham.

FIRST FLOOR (1,448 sq. ft.)

SECOND FLOOR (652 sq. ft.)

1155

GARDEN VIEW COTTAGE

Our Garden View Cottage is specially designed to capture light, breezes, and outdoor views. French doors topped by large fanlights flood the high-ceiling living room with light. A second window wall, in the dining room, overlooks the porch and rear garden.

Designed to use the full depth of the lot, the plan has an unusual layout that is basically one room deep. The plan's projections form protected L's at each end, which become natural locations for side courtyards. In mild climates, these courtyard L's serve as true outdoor rooms, increasing the pleasure and livability of the design. French doors at the front entry align with a second pair at the back of the house to create easy circulation between the two courtyards.

Practical as well as pretty, the house includes three bedrooms and 2½ baths in about 2,700 square feet of heated space. The downstairs master bedroom is airy and light filled, with vaulted ceiling, window bay, and French doors to the porch.

The kitchen includes a work/storage island, breakfast area, and a butler's pantry that leads to the dining room. Floors and countertops covered in white ceramic tile brighten the room.

Upstairs are two bedrooms and a shared compartment bath with separate vanities.

Formal details and special materials give the house its polished look. We suggest using a molded brick for house walls, a wood-shake roof, and a copper accent roof over the front latticed bay.

Although designed with deep, narrow lots in mind, the plan also is appropriate for larger, more conventional lots. Be sure to check local setback requirements.

Our Garden View Cottage was designed by Phillip Franks of Birmingham.

1161

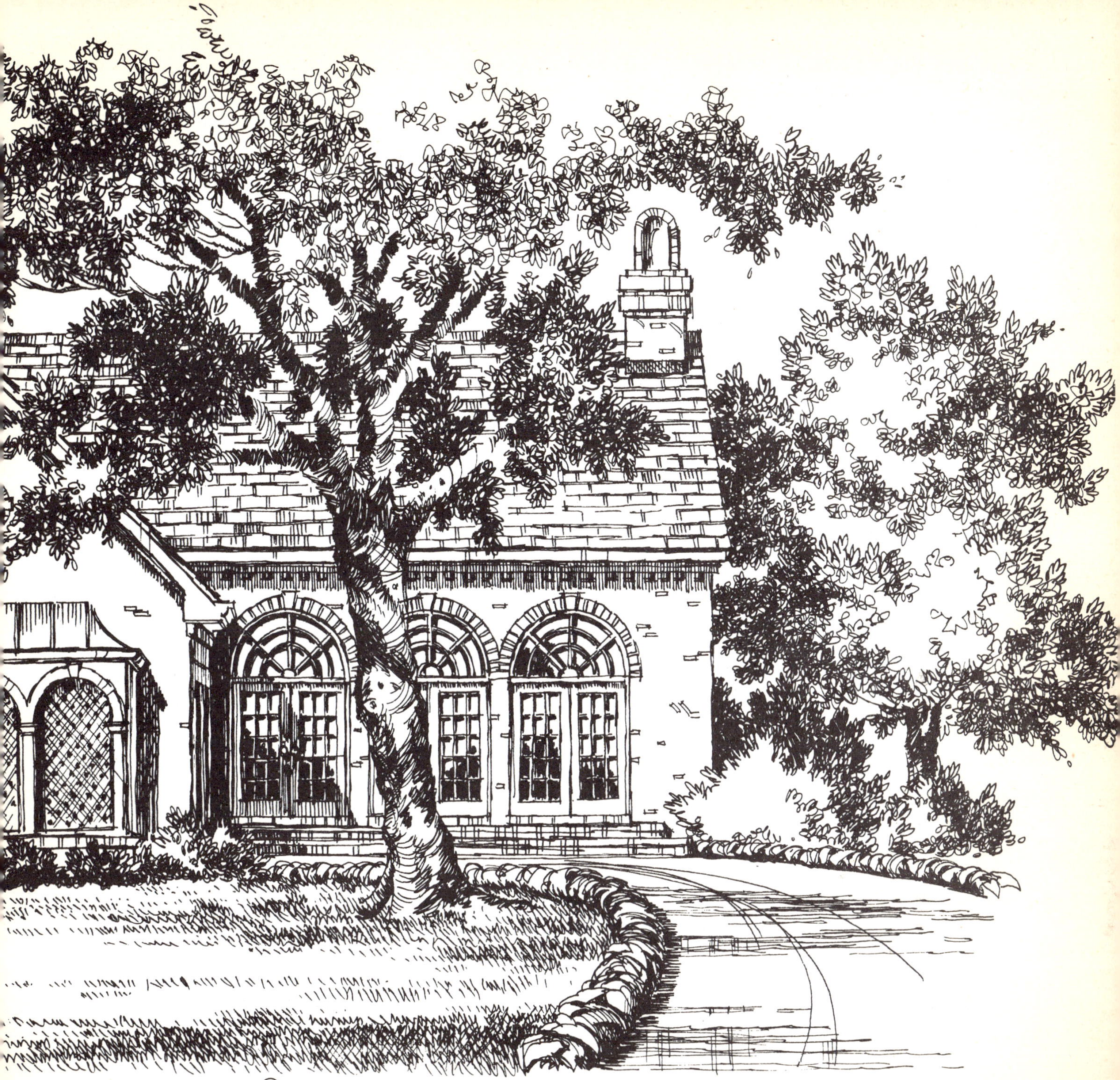

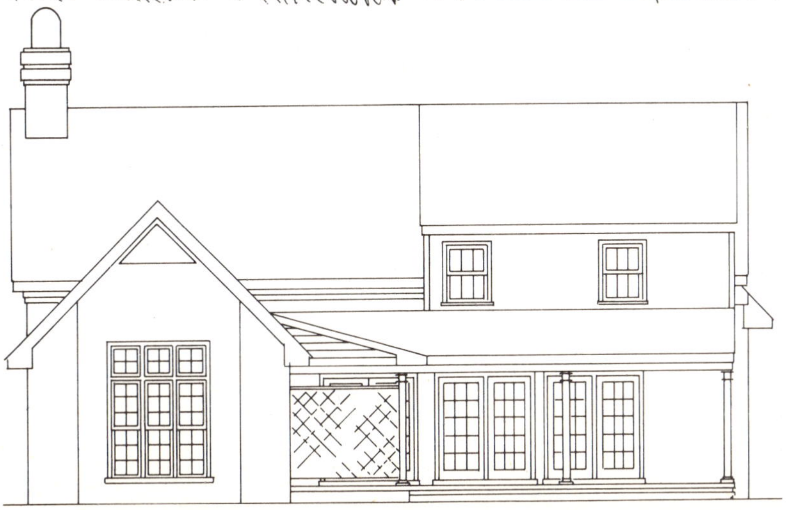

DOUBLE-GALLERY HOUSE

Double galleries dress the front of our French Colonial-style house. Simple Doric columns and a delicate diamond-patterned balustrade add classic detailing.

The house is adapted from a small plantation house in Point Coupée Parish, Louisiana. Like the original, our version is gracious rather than grand, containing about 3,700 square feet of heated space in two full stories. Galleries and terrace add almost 500 more square feet of living space.

The lower level is of stucco with wood clapboard above. A hipped roof with fanlight dormers reflects the French influence.

Inside is an expansive, comfortable plan with either 4 or 5 bedrooms and 3½ baths. A large family room with double-height ceiling occupies the center of the downstairs plan. The first floor also includes a spacious master bedroom with bath and formal living and dining rooms.

A peninsula divides the large working kitchen from the breakfast room. An old-fashioned butler's pantry and walk-in laundry add efficiency to the plan and also separate the dining room from the activity of the kitchen. A large terrace, accessible through four pairs of French doors, is located between the rear wings.

Upstairs, there are three bedrooms, one with a private bath. The two front bedrooms share a large compartment bath with double dressing areas.

The library/study forms a second living room for the area upstairs and is almost as large as the first-floor family room. It could serve as an additional bedroom. A balcony connects left and right portions of the upstairs plan and overlooks the family room. French doors open to the balcony on the front of the house.

Our Double-Gallery House was designed by Architect Bill Phillips, AIA, of Mobile.

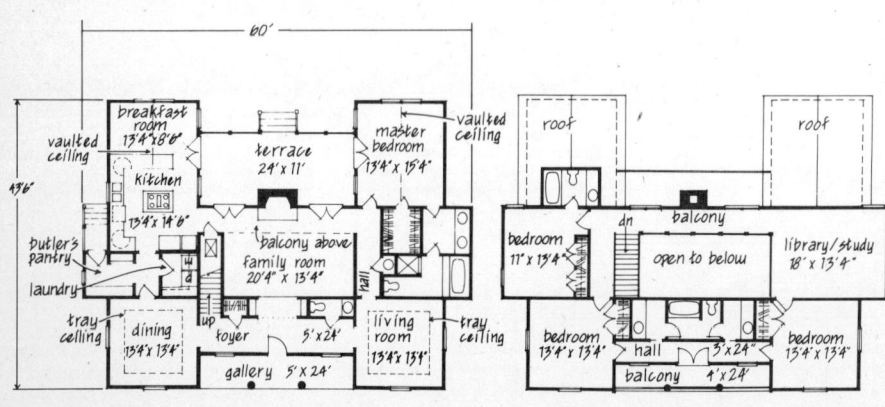

1153

VICTORIAN COTTAGE

With its gables, finials, brackets, and bays, our Victorian Cottage offers a lesson in turn-of-the-century design. Having overall dimensions of 36 x 46 feet, the house is suitable for a small lot in town, but its romantic, fanciful look would also make it ideal for a vacation home.

A pretty porte cochere creates a weatherproof welcome for visitors and also allows the placement of a graceful semicircular driveway. Carpenter detailing includes flower boxes at windows and airy latticework trim.

With about 1,900 square feet of heated space, the cottage is modest in size. Nine-foot ceilings downstairs give a feeling of spaciousness. Double French doors open the living room to a trellised pergola. In warm weather this arborlike structure becomes an extension of the living room.

The dining room is set into a deep bay and is designed to handle both family meals and formal dinners. Tall windows and a glass-paned door to the pergola brighten the room.

The downstairs is compact, and hallways are kept to a minimum. Tucked into the alcove under the stairs is a small area that can be used either as a study or for storage. It can be closed off with louvered doors.

Sloping ceilings add coziness and character to upstairs rooms. French doors set into an angled doorway open to the master bedroom, which has its own fireplace. A comfortable sitting room with vaulted ceiling is placed in the corner bay.

If desired, the two smaller bedrooms may be combined into one spacious room with adjoining bath.

We've specified moldings, mantels, and trim, but you may want to personalize the house with your own finds from antique shops and wrecking yards.

Our Victorian Cottage was designed by Frederick Spitzmiller and Robert Norris of Atlanta.

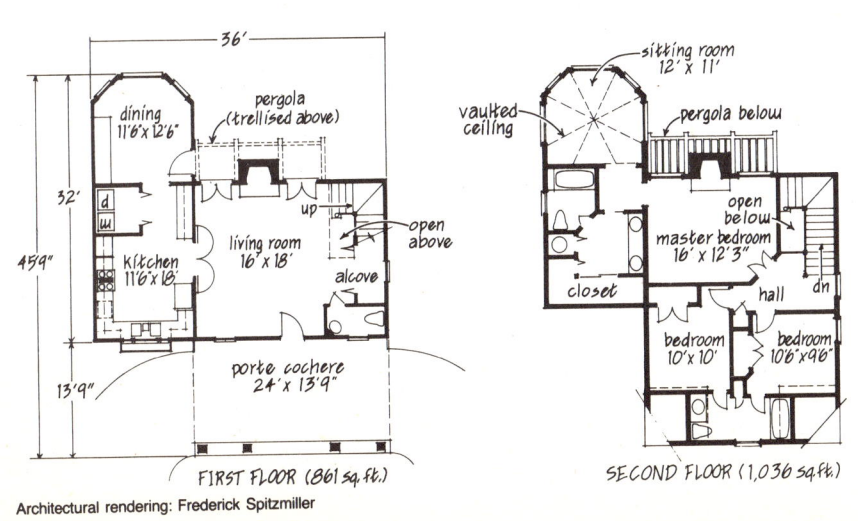

1157

Architectural rendering: Frederick Spitzmiller

FIRST FLOOR (861 sq. ft.)
SECOND FLOOR (1,036 sq. ft.)

WEEKENDER CABIN

Roughing it can be a lot of fun as our Weekender Cabin clearly shows. Ideal for short getaway trips or as a sportsman's cabin, it's also comfortable enough for more extended stays.

The cabin is perched on piers and clad in board-and-batten siding. We've detailed a simple stickwork balustrade. Following an early carpenter custom of personalizing a house, we've added a band of ship's wheel trim below the porch roof. Other trim designs may be chosen for your own signature.

The plan is simple, with the main area consisting of one large cooking, eating, and relaxing room. Off to the side, the bedroom is as snug as a ship's berth. It has a sloped ceiling, and the bed itself is tucked into a window bay. A small bath is behind the bedroom. A simple wood stove allows year-round use of the cabin.

There are less than 800 square feet of enclosed space, including an optional loft. A bank of windows and an angled bay expand the main living area. Front and back porches add almost 400 square feet of space.

Although the cabin is small, a circular stair gives access to a lofty crow's nest where the view is big. Two oversize porthole windows provide sweeping views of woods, lake, or ocean. The loft is a perfect place to set up a telescope or cots for younger guests. If extra sleeping space is needed, a screened porch offers room to hang a hammock.

The architect suggests a light blue-gray stain on the cabin, with railings and trim painted white for contrast and freshness. A metal roof of royal blue and a door painted terra-cotta remind owners and visitors that this is a getaway house—one meant for relaxing and fun.

To keep initial costs low, the interior walls can be left unfinished with a coat of whitewash on exposed framing. For a more finished look, beaded boards can be painted white or a washed blue. If a beach site is planned, be sure to check local ordinances and adapt foundation type and first-floor level accordingly.

Construction drawings include details for a marsh or dune walkover complete with simple shower and rinsing sink.

Our Weekender Cabin was designed by Architect Ron Haase, AIA, of Gainesville, Florida.

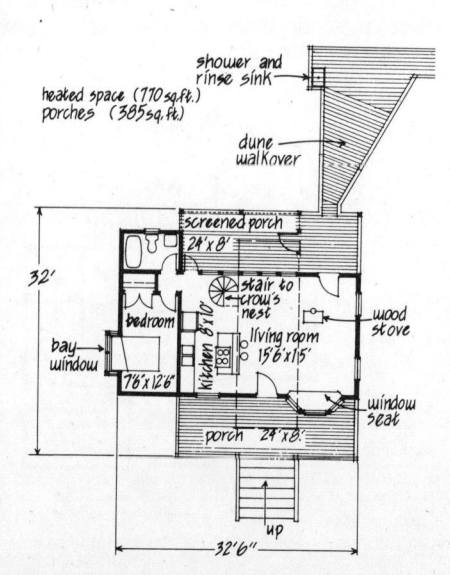

1156

CENTER GABLE COTTAGE

Our Center Gable Cottage combines a picturesque exterior with a compact, comfortable plan. Adapted from the Gothic Revival style popular in the mid-19th century, it features peaked gables, board-and-batten siding, and fanciful scroll-saw trim.

The house sits on a compact foundation (48 x 48 feet) and features a simple, but very livable, plan. It offers 3 bedrooms and 2½ baths in 3,000 square feet of space. The front porch adds about 350 square feet.

Downstairs, a semi-open plan includes a roomy master bedroom with adjoining bath and walk-in closet. A small vestibule separates the master bedroom from the rest of the downstairs.

With its double-height ceiling, French doors, and clerestory window placed high in the wall above, the dining room is a focal point for the plan. It overlooks the skylit sunroom, which can also serve as an informal family room.

In the kitchen, a triangular island divides the work area from the breakfast area. On both floors, halls are centered so that they become part of the living space rather than passageways.

Upstairs, two additional bedrooms share a roomy bath. Between the bedrooms, the hall forms a sitting room, which overlooks the dining room and also has a view to the back of the property.

Ceiling heights are 9 feet downstairs, 8 feet upstairs. Working drawings include a double garage (also in the Gothic Revival style), which is tied to the house by a covered breezeway.

Our Center Gable Cottage was designed by Phillip Franks of Birmingham.

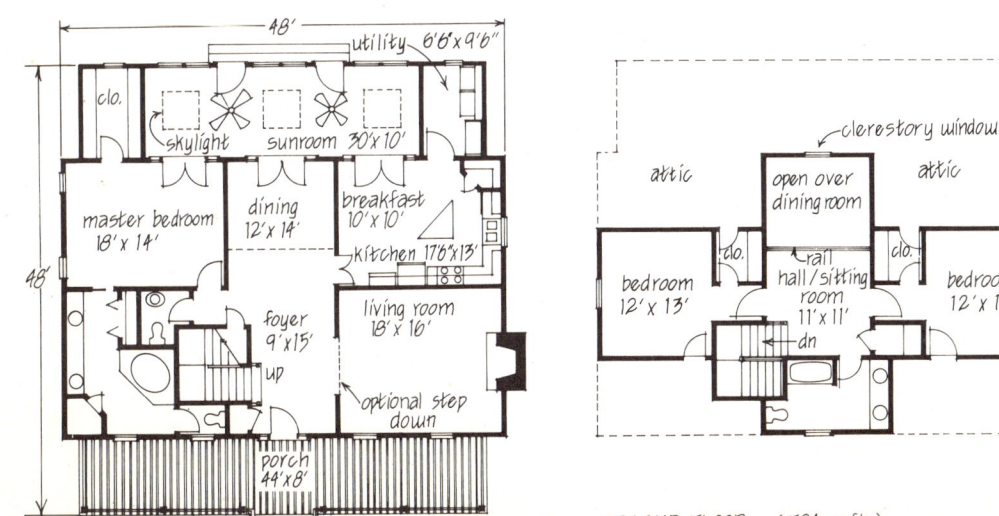

1159

CAROLINA COTTAGE

Our Carolina Cottage is based on one of the South's most familiar house types—the raised cottage. Commonly found along the Atlantic Coast and in the "sand hills" area between the Coastal Plain and the Piedmont, it is raised on piers and features a distinctive double-pitched roof.

In the back of the house, shed dormers, sometimes called "cat slides" in this part of the South, bring light to upstairs rooms. A double set of stairs with a center landing leads guests up to the front porch, and the large back porch can be screened.

House walls are of flush siding under the porches and lapped siding elsewhere. Chimney and support piers are masonry with a stucco finish. Walls can be stained a natural gray, and windows and doors painted antique red with soft-white trim.

The style of the house is "country formal," and the floor plan offers simple comfort. The plan is practical, too, with most rooms offering double use. The dining room doubles as a breakfast room; the living room can also serve as a more casual great room; and the downstairs bath is compartmentalized to double as a guest powder room.

The plan is compact, with short hallways and almost no wasted space. Storage is worked into nooks and recesses, and kitchen and baths are stacked adjacent to offer economy in construction.

The L-shaped kitchen is centered in the plan. It is compact but fully functional, with two walk-in pantries as well as additional storage.

Upstairs are two bedrooms, each with its own bath. Each bedroom has a dormer with window seat, as does the hall.

Our Carolina Cottage was designed by Architect Dean Winesett, AIA, of Hilton Head Island, South Carolina.

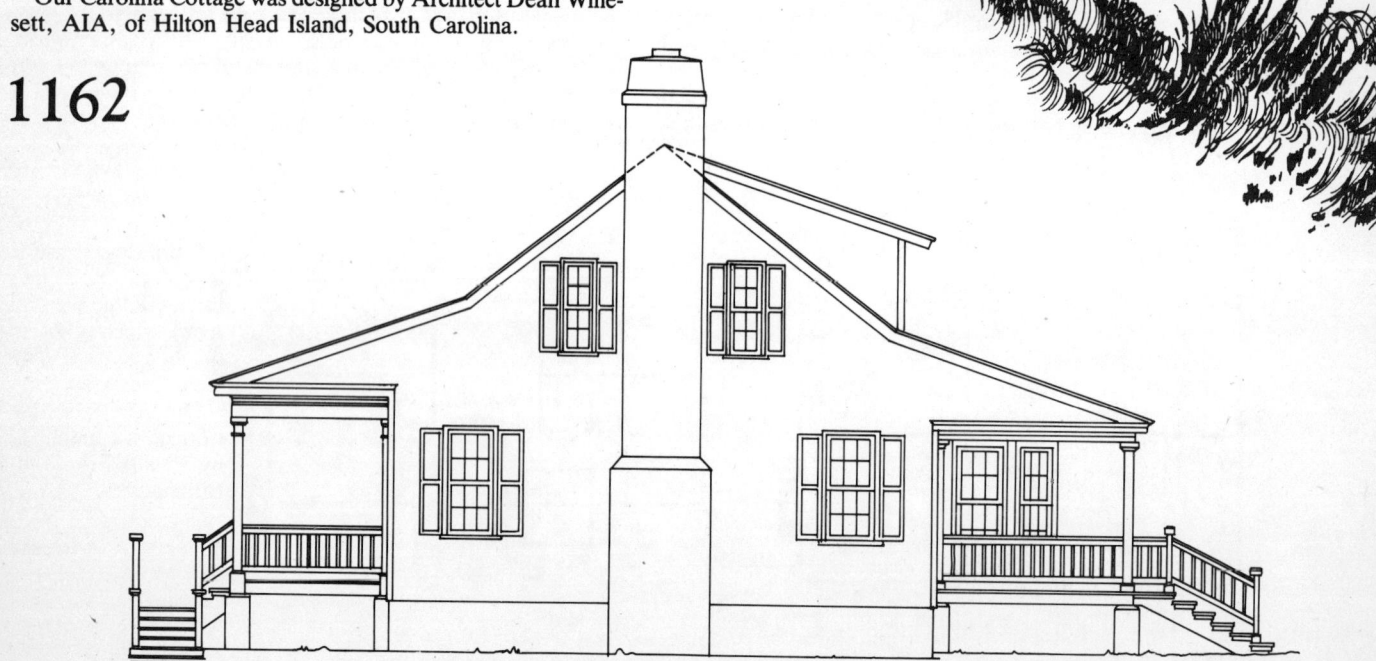

1162

FIRST FLOOR (1,266 sq. ft.)   SECOND FLOOR (711 sq. ft.)

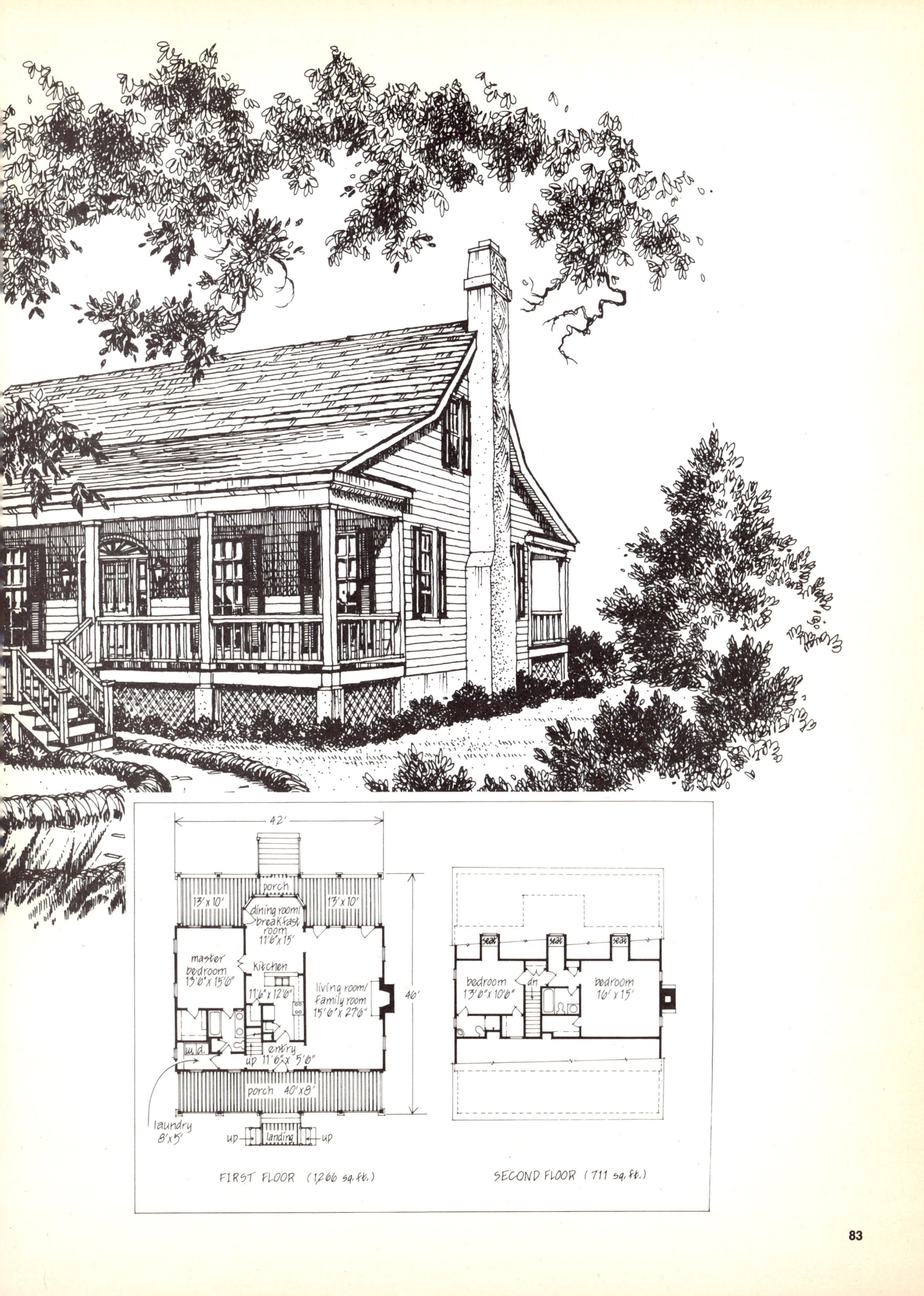

GREEK REVIVAL, VERNACULAR STYLE

Although many people associate the Greek Revival style with the white, columned plantation house, simpler, vernacular versions were much more typical. Pre-Civil War cottages, farmhouses, and even country stores all borrowed elements of the style.

This plan is based on one of the most common vernacular versions. It's a traditional two-story clapboard, containing about 3,000 square feet of space. A front-facing gable with a graceful "cobweb" fanlight echoes the pediment of the Greek temple. Corner pilasters replace the more typical (and costly) freestanding columns.

Inside is a large, old-fashioned great room with beamed ceiling and traditional mantel. The kitchen features a vaulted, beamed ceiling with skylights and an island work center. It adjoins a family breakfast area, which opens to a porch.

The separate dining room includes a true "china closet" and a box bay window. A combination powder room/bath allows the library to be converted into a guestroom.

Upstairs, the master bedroom features a tray ceiling and double sets of French doors, which open to a screened sitting porch. The master bath includes a large dressing area with walk-in cedar closet and separate bathtub and shower.

Across the hall, two additional bedrooms share a compartment bath. On the third level, double fan windows light the "bonus space," which could be an expansive studio, playroom, or retreat.

Our vernacular Greek Revival house was designed by G. John Baxter of Atlanta.

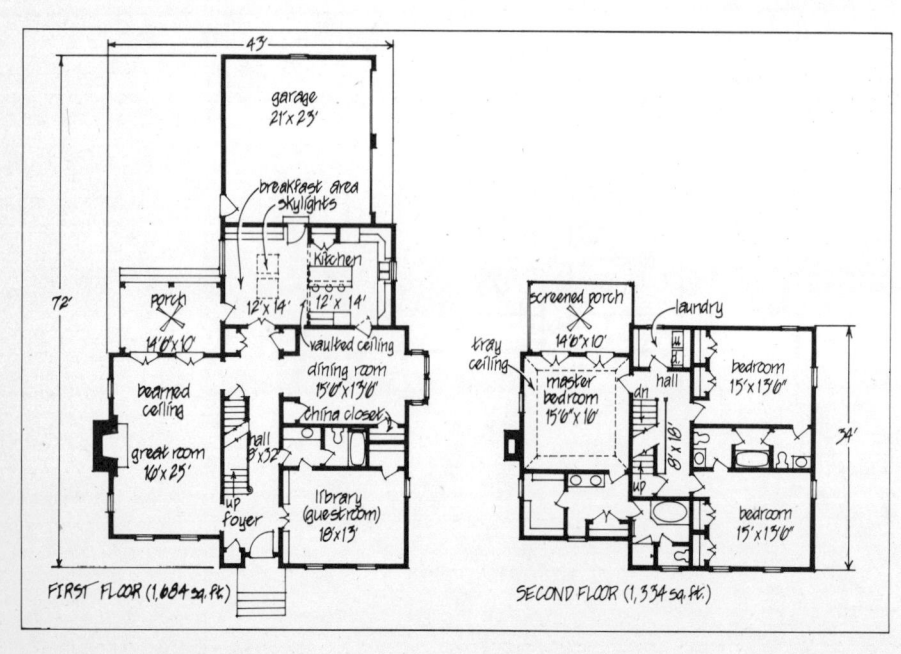

1170

SIMPLY SOUTHERN

Preserved from the past, this house plan is Simply Southern. Modeled after the I-House, a folk type widely found in the rural South in the 19th century, the design has country charm.

To suit the life-style of the Southern backcountry, the porch that once stretched along the front of the house was often enclosed at each end to make two small rooms. These were sometimes known as "prophet's chambers" because they provided ready accommodations for itinerant preachers and other travelers. This design element remains in our *Southern Living* version but with updated uses as a master bath and a study.

Designed by Phillip Franks of Birmingham, the plan is tall and narrow in profile. A gable roof covers the center of the house, which is skirted across the front and rear by one-story shed extensions. Its weathered-wood siding, twin brick chimneys, and a standing-seam metal roof project the feeling of the upland South.

Inside, rooms are spacious with 10-foot ceilings on the first floor and 9-foot ceilings upstairs. On both levels, rooms are arranged around the central staircase.

The first level is planned for efficiency. A cased opening links the foyer to the large living/family room. The study features two pairs of French doors, one leading into the living room and the other onto the front porch. The separate dining room is brightened by two pairs of fixed French windows and one pair of French doors, which open to the rear deck.

The bright, roomy kitchen includes an island work center and walk-in pantry. The skylit breakfast area is set in a deep boxed bay. The master bedroom contains a fireplace, spacious bath, and walk-in closet.

Upstairs, the hall forms a study area with space for a built-in desk. There are two bedrooms, each with its own bath.

Working drawings for this house include details for a double garage attached to the main house by a covered porch.

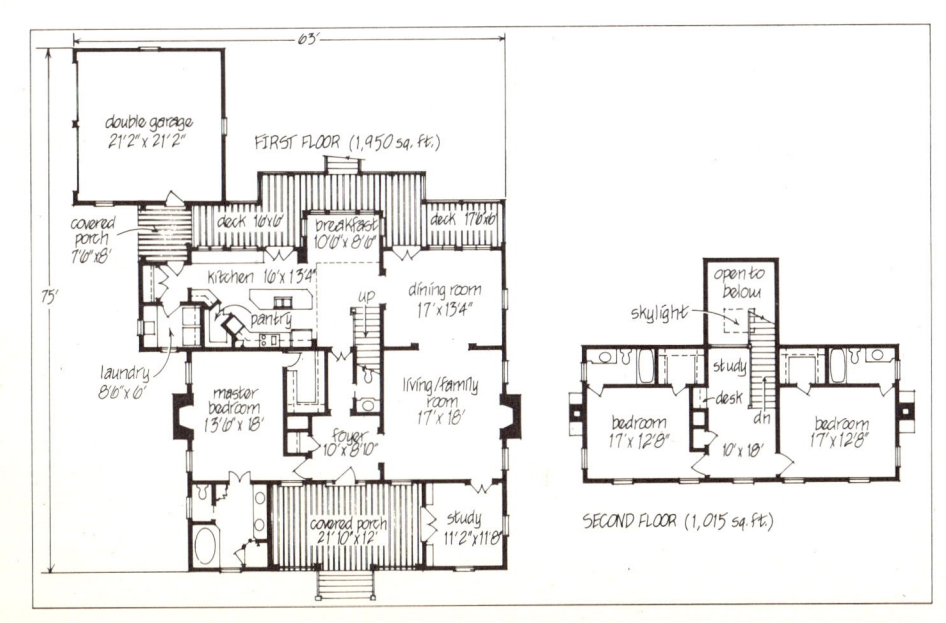

1171

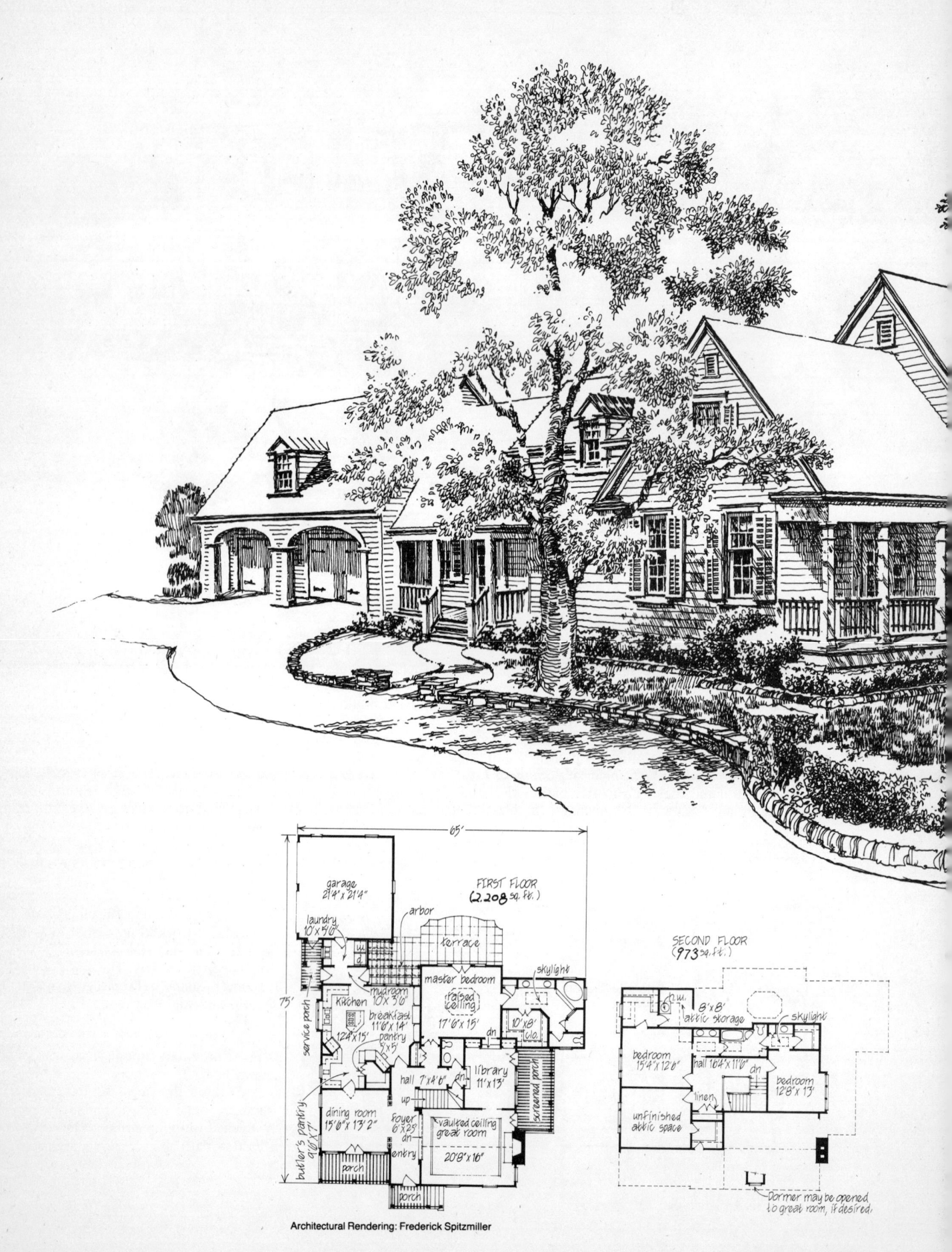

Architectural Rendering: Frederick Spitzmiller

COMFORTS OF A COLONIAL

Our Colonial-style cottage offers an appealing blend of comfort as well as history. Designed by Frederick Spitzmiller and Robert Norris of Atlanta, it's simply, but carefully, detailed with beaded weather-board walls, a shingle roof, and graceful columns with delicate wooden balustrades.

In the Colonial tradition, windows and doors get special attention: Quarter-round shutters and a fanlight decorate the doorway, and windows are framed by generous sills and lintels. There are 3 bedrooms and 2½ baths in over 3,100 square feet of heated space. A fourth bedroom could be added later in the unfinished attic space. (The 4-bedroom version contains just over 3,300 square feet.)

Downstairs, the master bedroom features a raised ceiling, large skylit bath, walk-in closet, and French doors leading to a terrace just outside. A small vestibule removes the master bedroom from the activity areas of the downstairs plan.

In the double-parlor tradition of many older homes, pocket doors open off the vaulted great room to a library. A second pair of pocket doors enables this room to function as a private sitting room for the master bedroom or as a guestroom.

The kitchen is a gathering spot for the house. It has two pantries, an island work center, and a built-in storage wall creating a family entertainment center. A desk with storage shelves above is angled into an alcove, with specialized storage for cookbooks and wine in the butler's pantry.

In the breakfast area, a window wall overlooks an L-shaped arbor. Tucked between terrace and garage, the arbor offers a shady alternative to the open terrace. French doors open to a small covered porch off the dining room and to a side screened porch off the great room and library. A practical mudroom, a laundry, and a service porch connect the house to its attached double garage.

Upstairs are two (or three) bedrooms and a compartment bath that has double dressing areas.

1164

FIRST FLOOR
(1,917 sq. ft.)

sunroom (optional)
14'6" x 11'0"

deck
12'0" x 12'0"

fan window on stair landing

breakfast
15' x 8'4"

family room
20'5" x 15'4"

tray ceiling

up dn
tray ceilings

master bedroom
15' x 15'

laundry
10'8" x 6'

dining room
14' x 15'4"

foyer
6' x 9'6"

living room
13'6" x 13'4"

pantry
4'4" x 6'

French doors

gallery 44' x 6'

SECOND FLOOR
(1,139 sq. ft.)

bedroom
12' x 15'

bedroom
12' x 11'

bedroom
13' x 15'

roof window

hall

roof window

roof

open to foyer

linen
4' x 5'

attic storage

88

LOUISIANA COUNTRY HOUSE

Our Louisiana Country House is built of stucco and cypress. The styling is classic provincial, with mullioned French doors opening to the front gallery and pyramid dormers punctuating the front of the roof.

The high, hipped roof flares slightly at the eaves and is covered in silvery cypress shingles. Six rustic columns, also of cypress, support the gallery roof.

The floor plan is simple but provides plenty of comfort, privacy, and flexibility. There are 4 bedrooms and 3½ baths in about 3,100 square feet of enclosed space. The sunroom (optional) contains an additional 180 square feet; gallery and deck more than 400 square feet.

Nine-foot ceilings, wide cased openings, and a double-height foyer give a spacious feeling to downstairs living areas. Angled French doors between the living room and the family room allow these rooms to work either separately or together.

The master bedroom, with tray ceiling and spacious master bath, is on the first floor. The kitchen, on the opposite side of the house, includes a separate breakfast area, an island work center, and an adjacent walk-in pantry.

A fan window (see sketch) graces the stair landing. Upstairs are three bedrooms and two baths. Construction drawings include a basement plan with double garage.

Our Louisiana Country House was designed by Phillip Franks of Birmingham.

1165

ISLAND-STYLE HOUSE

A whimsical sunburst in the porch gable welcomes guests to our casual Island-Style House. Underscoring the easygoing tropical look are walls of pastel-painted stucco accented by fresh white trim.

A shady porch wraps the house and creates a protective, cool zone during hot, Southern summers. A pyramid roof of Bermuda-style steel shingles covers the house and porches while leaving the courtyard behind the house open to sunshine.

The flexible, one-level plan can be built at two different square footages. If the master bedroom wing is included, the house offers three bedrooms and about 2,000 square feet of space. If built as a two-bedroom house, there are about 1,500 square feet of space. Porches and courtyard add another 1,100 square feet.

The living room is large, 18½ x 23½ feet. It appears even larger because it's open to the foyer, kitchen, and breakfast room. French doors flank the fireplace and open to the rear porch and courtyard.

The master bedroom occupies its own wing at the rear of the plan. A private entry porch and small sitting porch give it the feeling of a separate apartment.

The large kitchen includes an island in the center. Wide-slat plantation shutters above a second island screen the kitchen from the living room. A separate dining room includes a pass-through butler's pantry as well as French doors to the side porch.

We've tucked a miniature outdoor kitchen with small refrigerator and built-in grill into the corner of the back porch for the convenience of outdoor parties. An airy latticed wall screens the rear courtyard.

The detailing of the portico can be individualized, and we've included an alternate design, fully screened with lattice, in our working drawings.

Our Island-Style House was designed by Tim Holmes of Watson Watson Rutland/Architects Inc., located in Montgomery, Alabama.

three-bedroom option — 1,964 sq. ft.
two-bedroom option — 1,559 sq. ft.
porches and courtyard — 1,120 sq. ft.

1158

A CONTEMPORARY CLASSIC

On the front gable, a carved, decorative swag dresses our Contemporary Classic house. A graceful porch extends a warm Southern welcome.

Designed by Frederick Spitzmiller and Robert Norris of Atlanta, the house combines traditional styling with a comfortable and more contemporary floor plan.

The house plan features a story-and-a-half center section and two single-story wings. Outside, pale, stucco walls; a white, wooden portico; and dark-green shutters emphasize the look of tradition.

Inside, the floor plan is traditional but updated. Wide cased openings off the center hall and between the dining room and great room take the place of conventional doors. As a result, the hall, living room, dining room, and great room open to each other.

The kitchen includes both "in line" and island work centers, a breakfast area, walk-in pantry, laundry, and mudroom.

The master bedroom has a tray ceiling, roomy closet space, and French doors leading to the rear terrace. Upstairs, there are two more bedrooms, each with a dormer window. The rooms share a connecting bath.

Our Contemporary Classic house contains about 3,000 square feet of heated space; porches and terrace contain over 400 square feet.

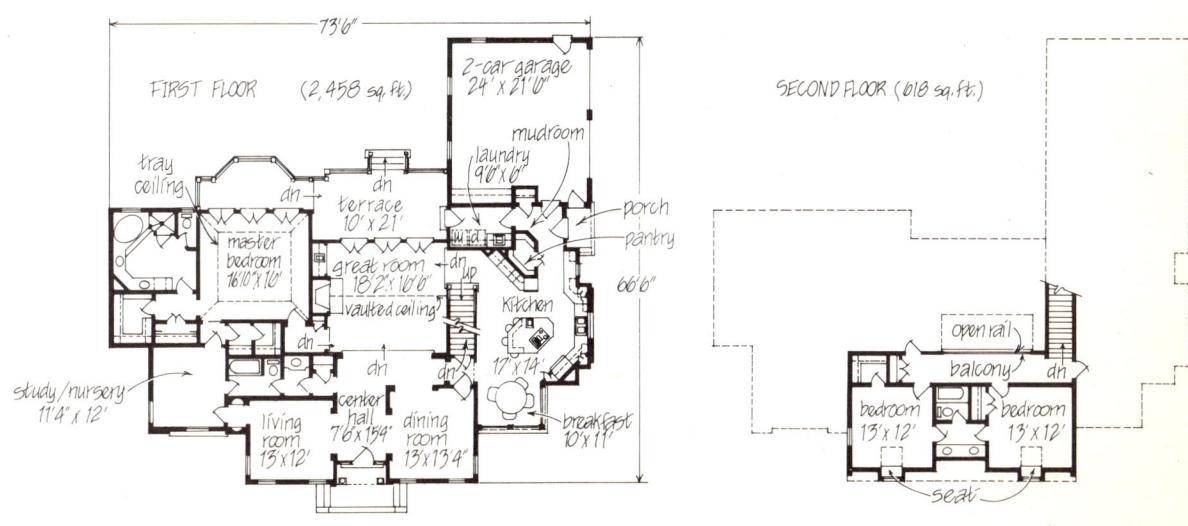

Architectural rendering: Frederick Spitzmiller

1166

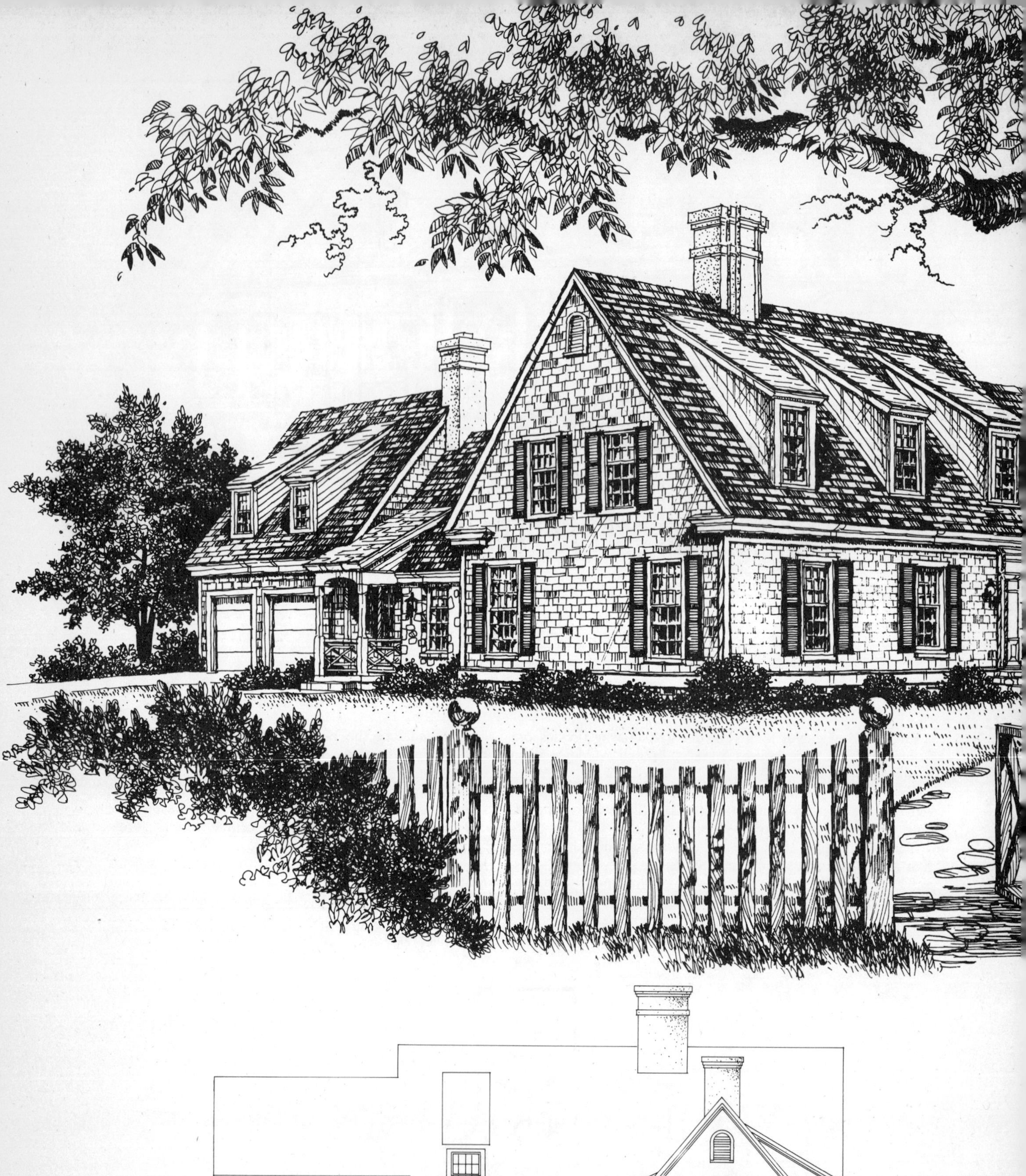

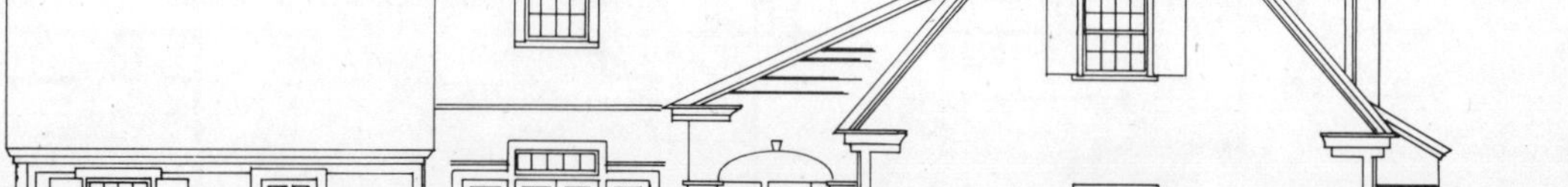

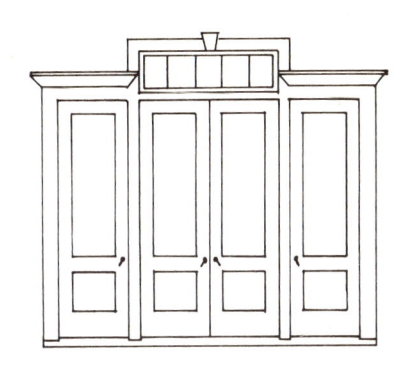

SHINGLE-STYLE COTTAGE

Walls of cedar shingles and weathered fieldstone give the cozy look of a country cottage to this house plan. Twelve-over-twelve windows framed by functioning shutters emphasize its authentic colonial character.

Designed by G. John Baxter of Atlanta, the plan contains approximately 3,100 square feet of space with additional living space in porches and deck. An optional fourth bedroom and bath in the "bonus" space above the garage would bring the total square footage to about 3,450.

Although simple and colonial in spirit, the design offers a number of polished details. Fluted pilasters frame the six-panel door, and a cluster of chimney stacks accents the gabled roof. Corner boards, cornice, and other exterior moldings are carefully detailed to give the house a historic look.

The living room is centered in the plan and features a formal fireplace with paneled overmantel. French doors with a transom open to a spacious sun deck. A skylit porch tucked between living and family rooms creates a shady sitting area.

The master bedroom features a tray ceiling, graceful fan window, double walk-in closets, and an ample bath. Private access to the sun deck is through the dressing area.

The kitchen includes an island work center and opens to a combination breakfast/family room with vaulted ceiling, fireplace, and built-in bookcases.

The upstairs has two large bedrooms, each with its own bath and dormer window seat.

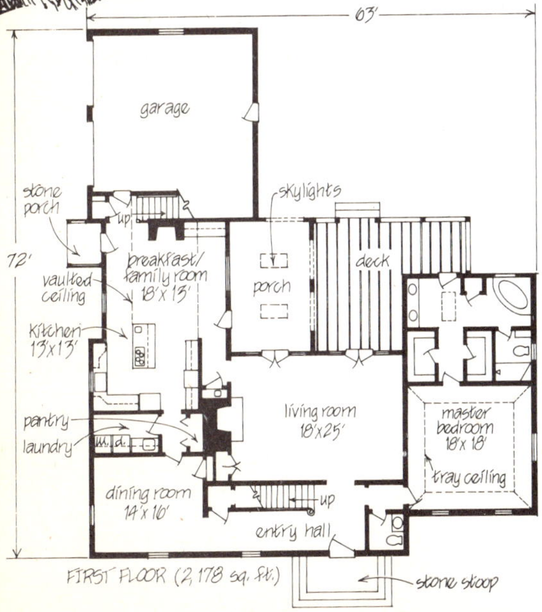

1167

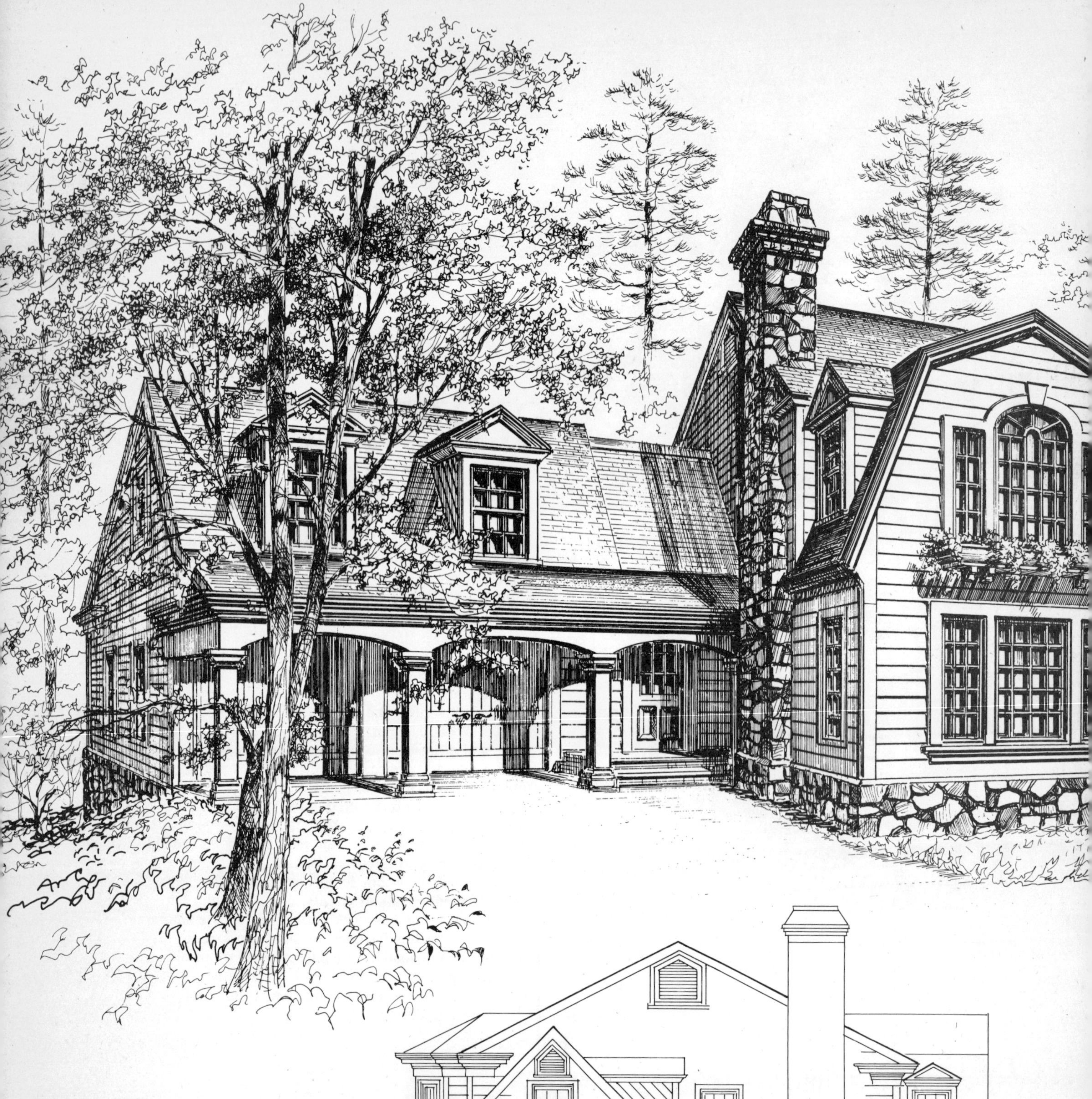

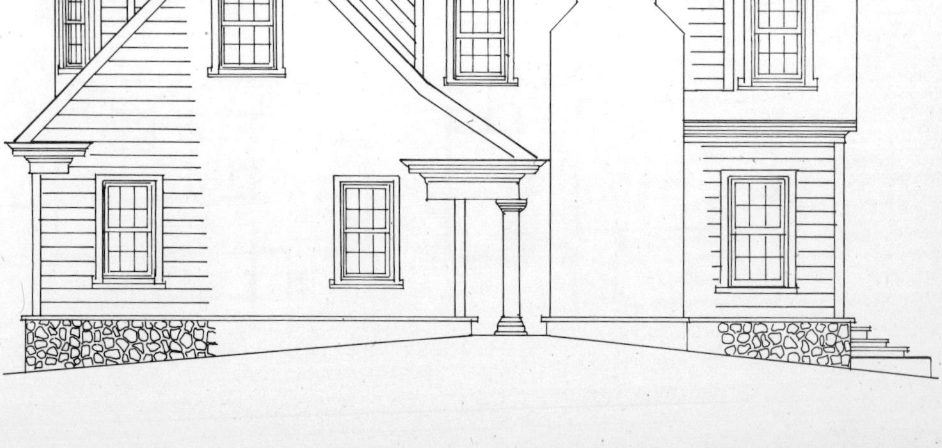

A COUNTRY HOUSE FOR SADDLEBROOK

From its gambrel roof to its stone chimney and charming cottage window boxes, our Saddlebrook House brims with country character.

The house features either three or four bedrooms and three baths in about 3,100 square feet of heated space. The "bonus" room above the garage yields more than 300 square feet of additional space. The unfinished basement offers almost 700 square feet for an extra bedroom, bath, and playroom.

Cottage characteristics inside include a homey, paneled great room with 9-foot beamed ceiling, stone fireplace, and hearth. French doors with wide-slat plantation louvers are throughout the house.

The kitchen opens to a spacious breakfast room, which in turn opens to a deck. A separate dining room and guest bedroom/study complete the first-floor plan.

A mudroom and walk-in laundry connect the house and garage; plank doors and old-fashioned hardware give the attached double garage the look of a stable.

Upstairs, the master bedroom is comfortable and private. Although spacious (23 x 16 feet) with a vaulted ceiling, it continues the cozy, cottage look. Window seats flank a stone fireplace, and a large fan window frames views to the outside. French doors lead to a master bath with bathing bay, separate shower, and double walk-in closets. Across the hall are two additional bedrooms with a shared bath.

Steve Fuller of Design Traditions, Inc., of Atlanta, designed the Saddlebrook House.

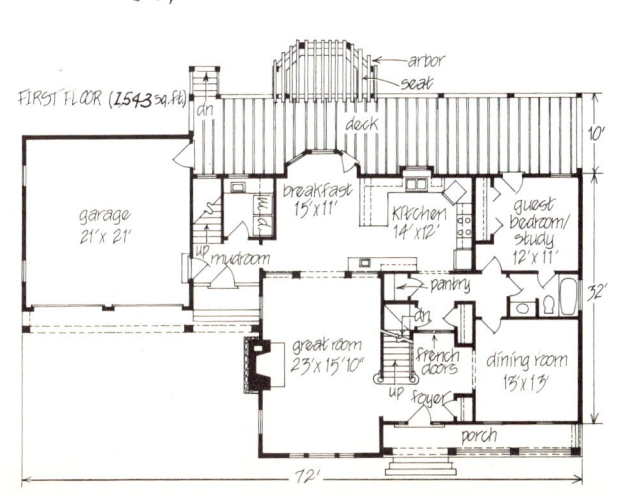

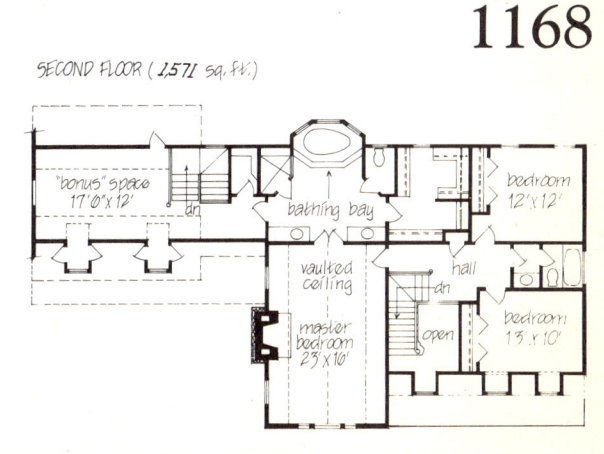

1168

INDEX OF HOUSE PLANS

All-Seasons House, An (1119)..................42	Galleries Cool Our Gulf Coast Cottage (1131).......... 50
Always Wanted a Gazebo? (1112)......................... 28	Garden View Cottage (1161)................................ 76
Budget Beach House (1102)................................. 15	Greek Revival, Vernacular Style (1170)................ 84
Build a Tradition (1111)...................................... 26	House for Comfort and Tradition, A (1137).......... 58
Cape Cod, Southern Style (1117).........................17	House for Town or Country, A (1115)................... 27
Carolina Cottage (1162)...................................... 82	House in Three Parts, A (1126)............................ 46
Carpenter Cottage (1124).................................... 48	Island-Style House (1158)....................................90
Center Gable Cottage (1159)............................... 81	Kennesaw Country House (1154)..........................73
Chesapeake Country Home (1141).......................64	Live the Country Life (1144)................................ 66
Classic Country Farmhouse, A (1125)................. 44	Louisiana Country House (1165).........................88
Classic in Two Sizes, A (1134)............................ 54	Lowlands House, Our (1149)................................ 67
Classic Villa (1152)... 69	Mixing Simplicity with Style (1113)...................... 25
Coastal Cottage (1110).. 24	North Florida Cottage (1150)............................... 72
Come Home to a Classic (1121).......................... 38	Piedmont House, Our (1151)................................ 70
Comforts of a Colonial (1164).............................86	Plan for Indoor and Outdoor Living, A (1118).......... 34
Contemporary Cabin (1103)................................ 18	Porches Add Polish (1143).................................. 62
Contemporary Classic, A (1166).......................... 91	Rustic Farmhouse, A (1129)................................ 49
Cottage of Sticks and Stones, A (1108)...................20	Shingle-Style Cottage (1167)................................ 92
Country English—In Town (1172)........................30	Simply Southern (1171).......................................85
Country Farmhouse (1135)................................. 55	Sloop Point Farmhouse (1120).............................36
Country Georgian (1116).................................... 32	Small House with Appeal (1132)........................... 52
Country House for Saddlebrook, A (1168)............. 94	Stone Accents Stucco in Our
Courtyard Garden House (1127)..........................43	Courtyard Home (1142)................................... 60
Courtyard House, A (1104)................................. 16	Texas-Style Farmhouse, A (1169)........................ 31
Creole Cottage Blends Traditions (1109).................. 22	Tidewater Traditional, A (1123)........................... 35
Deck House That's Small but Special, A (1106)....... 19	Traditional Williamsburg (1136)...........................56
Details Make the Difference (1122).......................40	Two-for-One House (1148)...................................68
Double-Gallery House (1153)...............................78	Vernacular Cottage (1101).................................. 14
Florida Garden House (1133)...............................53	Victorian Cottage (1157)..................................... 79
Four Porches House (1155)................................. 74	Virginia House, Our (1139)................................. 61
French Country House, A (1146).........................65	Weekender Cabin (1156)......................................80
Galleries, The (1105)...12	Williamsburg Home, Our (1138)..........................57

ABOUT OUR PLANS

Our plans are full working drawings and include foundation and floor-framing plans; dimensioned floor plans; electrical plans; typical wall section; exterior elevations of the front, sides, and rear of house; interior elevations; door and window schedules; and suggested exterior and interior finish schedules.

Due to regional variations in climate and in building codes, heating and plumbing plans should be supplied by the local subcontractors. Similarly, we recommend that material quantity lists, such as lumber lists, be obtained from the contractor or from the local supplier.

Our architects design all our plans to meet the requirements of the Southern Building Code, but because codes are subject to change and varying interpretations, we cannot warrant compliance with any specific codes and ordinances. Your local builder must review the plan and ensure that it complies with all applicable building codes and is suitable for your particular site, including any subdivision restrictions. Because we have no control over the selection of your builder or other professionals, we cannot be responsible for the advice or assistance you receive from them, or for the methods they use.

Note: Our square footage estimates are based on inside room dimensions. They are approximations. Accurate construction-cost estimates should be taken from the blueprints and should include exterior wall thicknesses.

Reverse Orders

Sometimes, to better site a house, builders require a reverse set of plans (often called a mirror image or flopped set). The lettering and dimensions will appear backward on the reverse set. If you need a reverse set of plans, specify one reverse set and the rest standard sets of plans. There is an additional charge of $25 for a reverse order. For example, to order one reverse and four regular sets, the cost would be $200 plus $25, or $225 total. The cost of one regular and one reverse set would be $150 plus $30 plus $25, or $205 total.

SOUTHERN LIVING PLANS®
Box C-349
Birmingham, Alabama 35283

CREDIT CARD ORDERS, CALL TOLL FREE
1-800-633-8628. (AL. residents, call 1-800-292-8667.)

1 set	$150
5 sets	$200
each additional (after initial order)	$ 30
reverse set order	$ 25
Alabama residents please add 4% state sales tax	$____
TOTAL PRICE	$____

SOUTHERN LIVING PLANS®
Box C-349 Birmingham, Alabama 35283

Please send me _____ set(s) of plan # _____,
_____ reverse set(s) (if applicable). TOTAL $_____
CREDIT CARD ORDERS, CALL TOLL FREE
1-800-633-8628. (AL. residents, call 1-800-292-8667.)

Name _____
Street Address _____
City _____
State _____
Zip _____
Daytime Phone # ( ) _____
_____ Visa _____ MasterCard _____ American Express
Card # _____
Card Expires _____
Signature _____

SOUTHERN LIVING PLANS®
Box C-349 Birmingham, Alabama 35283

Please send me _____ set(s) of plan # _____,
_____ reverse set(s) (if applicable). TOTAL $_____
CREDIT CARD ORDERS, CALL TOLL FREE
1-800-633-8628. (AL. residents, call 1-800-292-8667.)

Name _____
Street Address _____
City _____
State _____
Zip _____
Daytime Phone # ( ) _____
_____ Visa _____ MasterCard _____ American Express
Card # _____
Card Expires _____
Signature _____

SOUTHERN LIVING PLANS®
Box C-349 Birmingham, Alabama 35283

Please send me _____ set(s) of plan # _____,
_____ reverse set(s) (if applicable). TOTAL $_____
CREDIT CARD ORDERS, CALL TOLL FREE
1-800-633-8628. (AL. residents, call 1-800-292-8667.)

Name _____
Street Address _____
City _____
State _____
Zip _____
Daytime Phone # ( ) _____
_____ Visa _____ MasterCard _____ American Express
Card # _____
Card Expires _____
Signature _____

SOUTHERN LIVING PLANS®
Box C-349 Birmingham, Alabama 35283

Please send me _____ set(s) of plan # _____,
_____ reverse set(s) (if applicable). TOTAL $_____
CREDIT CARD ORDERS, CALL TOLL FREE
1-800-633-8628. (AL. residents, call 1-800-292-8667.)

Name _____
Street Address _____
City _____
State _____
Zip _____
Daytime Phone # ( ) _____
_____ Visa _____ MasterCard _____ American Express
Card # _____
Card Expires _____
Signature _____